THE ACTION BIBLE
DEVOTIONAL

THE ACTION BIBLE DEVOTIONAL

52 WEEKS OF GOD-INSPIRED ADVENTURE

JEREMY V. JONES

ILLUSTRATIONS BY SERGIO CARIELLO

THE ACTION BIBLE GENERAL EDITOR DOUG MAUSS

David C Cook
transforming lives together

THE ACTION BIBLE DEVOTIONAL
Published by David C Cook
4050 Lee Vance View
Colorado Springs, CO 80918 U.S.A.

David C Cook Distribution Canada
55 Woodslee Avenue, Paris, Ontario, Canada N3L 3E5

David C Cook U.K., Kingsway Communications
Eastbourne, East Sussex BN23 6NT, England

The graphic circle C logo is a registered trademark of David C Cook.

Scripture quotations marked NLT are taken from the *Holy Bible*, New Living Translation,
copyright © 1996, 2007 by Tyndale House Foundation. Used by permission of
Tyndale House Publishers, Inc., Carol Stream, Illinois 60188. All rights reserved;
NIV are taken from the Holy Bible, New International Version®, NIV®. Copyright ©
1973, 1984 by Biblica, Inc.™ Used by permission of Zondervan. All rights reserved
worldwide. www.zondervan.com; NCV are taken from the New Century Version®.
Copyright © 2005 by Thomas Nelson, Inc. Used by permission. All rights reserved.

LCCN 2012936140
ISBN 978-0-7814-0727-4
eISBN 978-1-4347-0509-9

© 2012 David C Cook
The Action Bible text © 2010 David C Cook
The Action Bible illustrations © 2010 Sergio Cariello

The Action Bible Bible Editor: Shawn Yost, M. Div.
The Action Bible Letterers: Dave Lanphear, Dave Rothe
The Action Bible Colorists: Patrick Gama, and
Wellington Marçal, Priscila Ribeiro, Fabrício Sampaio Guerra,
MaxFlan Araujo, Alex Guim of Impacto Studio

The Team: Don Pape, Susan Tjaden, Amy Konyndyk, Renada Arens
Cover Design: Nick Lee
Cover Illustrations: Sergio Cariello

Printed in the United States of America
First Edition 2012

1 2 3 4 5 6 7 8 9 10

051612

AND ... ACTION!

The Bible can be intimidating. It's okay; you can admit it. I mean, it's got *all* those words in tiny print packed across the pages. It's a good thing *The Action Bible* came along!

People say a picture is worth a thousand words, right? *The Action Bible* is all about the pictures—cool pictures, comic pictures. And those pictures bring the stories of the Bible to life in whole new colorful ways, without having to use *so many* words. You can see the action jump off the page. You can understand the stories much more easily. And all that helps you bring the power of the Bible to life in your everyday world.

See, that's the thing about the Bible—it's way more than just another book. It's God's book. God wants His Word to come alive in our heads so we understand His ways. He wants it to come alive in our hearts so we feel His presence. And He wants it to come alive in our hands and feet so we live it out and experience it—that means action. Not action that just means following a list of dos and don'ts. Not trying to impress God by following all the rules. It's way better than that.

It means …

+ diving into God's story and seeing that He still performs superhero feats.

+ going from bored to bold.

+ stepping out and joining God for great adventures in your life.

Action shows that we really believe what we say we believe. It helps us experience God and get to know Him better. Jesus wants us to think about and feel our faith deeply. But He also wants followers willing to go with Him on exciting adventures. He wants us to get our hands dirty. Adventure can be a little risky sometimes. You might not be able to see what's coming next. You'll run into obstacles. But the rewards are so cool. Going on God's adventures helps us see firsthand that He's still able to do superhero feats in our lives. How amazing is that?

So How Do You Use This Book?

It's easy—and fun. Every week this year, you get …

+ one cool illustrated story from *The Action Bible*.

+ Key Verse: We used a bunch of different Bible translations, but you can look it up in your own Bible and read more in the translation you like to use.

+ X-Ray Vision: some short thoughts to connect the story with your life.

+ Your Mission: three ideas to put the themes into action! Pick one or try all three.

+ Your Debrief: three questions to spark some brain cells.

+ Mission Accomplished: your place to make some notes to remember.

+ Share the Adventure: occasional ideas to involve parents or friends.

+ Big Picture Page: occasional pages for you to get creative. Write. Draw. Tape and stick. Take the idea and run wild with it.

Your Book, Your Adventure

Sound like a lot? Don't worry. You've got all week. And you've got options. Do a little each day. And use this book however you want—just use it. Dive into the adventure. Read the stories. Accept the missions. Dream up your own. Talk to God about them. Try them. Read more in *The Action Bible* and more in your usual Bible.

This is your book. You get to chart your own action expeditions with God's help. So what are you waiting for? All great adventures start with the first step. Let's go!

In the Beginning ...

... THERE WAS NOTHING.

EXCEPT GOD.

Day 1

GOD'S SPIRIT MOVED THROUGH THE VOID. THEN GOD SPOKE:

LET THERE BE LIGHT!

Day 2

THEN GOD SEPARATED THE WATERS OF THE NOTHINGNESS INTO THE MOISTURE AND CLOUDS OF THE SKY ABOVE, AND THE DROPS AND WAVES OF THE OCEAN BELOW. GOD NAMED THE SKY "HEAVENS."

Day 3

GOD NAMED THE LOWER WATERS THE "SEA." HE GATHERED TOGETHER THE WATERS OF THE SEA, EXPOSING DRY GROUND. HE NAMED THE DRY LAND "EARTH." ON THIS LAND, HE MADE GRASS AND FLOWERS AND TREES. HE MADE THEM WITH SEEDS SO THEY COULD GROW MORE GRASS AND FLOWERS AND TREES. THE FRUITFUL EARTH WAS A PLACE OF BEAUTY.

AND GOD KNEW THAT IT WAS GOOD.

Day 4

THEN GOD FASHIONED THE SUN, THE MOON, AND THE STARS TO LIGHT THE EARTH. AND HE SET THEM IN THE HEAVENS TO MARK THE DAYS, SEASONS, AND YEARS.

Day 5

GOD SAID, "LET THE WATER BE FILLED WITH LIVING CREATURES!" AND THE SEAS AND RIVERS SWARMED WITH WHALES AND FISH.

GOD SAID, "LET BIRDS FLY THROUGH THE SKY." AND THE OPEN SKY ABOVE THE EARTH WAS FILLED WITH EVERY KIND OF FLYING BIRD.

"BE FRUITFUL AND FILL THE EARTH," GOD SAID AS HE BLESSED THE LIVING CREATURES OF THE SEA AND SKY.

AND GOD KNEW THAT IT WAS GOOD.

Day 6

THEN GOD SAID, "LET THE EARTH BRING FORTH LIVING CREATURES." AND GOD MADE ALL KINDS OF ANIMALS: WILD ONES, TAME ONES—EVEN THOSE THAT CRAWL ON THE GROUND.

THEN GOD CREATED THE FIRST MAN, ADAM, AND THE FIRST WOMAN, EVE. THEY WERE THE GREATEST OF ALL GOD'S CREATIONS BECAUSE HE MADE THEM IN HIS OWN IMAGE, TO BE A REFLECTION OF WHAT HE IS LIKE. GOD MADE ADAM AND EVE WITH SOULS THAT WOULD LIVE FOREVER. AND HE PLANNED FOR PEOPLE TO RULE AND LIVE IN HARMONY WITH EVERY LIVING THING ON EARTH.

GOD LOOKED AT EVERYTHING THAT HE HAD MADE, AND HE KNEW IT WAS ALL VERY, VERY GOOD.

Day 7

AND ON THE SEVENTH DAY, GOD RESTED.

GOD SHOWED ADAM AND EVE THE BEAUTY AND FRUITFULNESS OF THE GARDEN THEY LIVED IN. HE TOLD THEM, "YOU MAY EAT FROM EVERY TREE EXCEPT ONE, THE TREE OF KNOWLEDGE OF GOOD AND EVIL. IF YOU EAT FROM THAT TREE, YOU WILL DIE."

IN THE BEGINNING ...

KEY VERSE

THEN GOD LOOKED OVER ALL HE HAD MADE, AND HE SAW THAT IT WAS VERY GOOD!

—Genesis 1:31 NLT

X-RAY VISION

You know what's crazy? Salmon swim up rivers and rapids to the exact same spot they were born. Birds fly thousands of miles each year to find the best weather, food, and nests—some butterflies do that too. The ocean is so big we still don't know everything that's in it. No two snowflakes are exactly alike. (Think about how many billions of snowflakes there must be in a single blizzard!) The sun is about 28 million degrees Fahrenheit at its core, but it never burns up.

You've probably learned some amazing nature facts in school. God created all that amazing stuff. Think about it: He turned nothing into everything! His creativity is all around us—no matter if we live in Yosemite National Park or Park Podunk in the desert.

But it's easy for us to get so used to it all that we don't think twice about the creation in our own backyards. We get stuck in front of our video games and screens, and we forget there's a real world way cooler than HD—and a Creator who's way more powerful than any action hero. Sometimes we need the wild to give us a wake-up call. We need a reminder about just how ginormous and mind-blowing our God is.

YOUR MISSION

1. Go outside. Look around and write down the miracles of creation you see—even if they're all in your backyard or local park.

2. Read Psalm 19 out loud, outside.

3. Stargaze. Stare into the night sky from your deck.

YOUR DEBRIEF

- What's the most amazing thing in nature you've ever seen?

- What does creation make you feel about God?

- How big do you think God is?

MISSION ACCOMPLISHED

What did you learn?

What do you want to remember?

SHARE THE ADVENTURE

Get moving. Go with your parents to explore a local hiking trail or walking path. Climb a mountain or the highest hill in town. At the very least, walk around the block with your eyes and ears wide open to what God has made.

TEMPTED IN THE GARDEN

WEEK 2

KEY VERSE

AND THE LORD GOD MADE CLOTHING FROM ANIMAL SKINS FOR ADAM AND HIS WIFE.

God forgives us and will always take care of us no matter what.

—Genesis 3:21 NLT

X-RAY VISION

Doh! You did it again! You didn't really mean to. You swore you wouldn't fight with your brother again. You promised you'd never lie to your parents again. You vowed not to talk behind a friend's back again. But, uh, it just kind of … happened.

None of us is perfect. We all make bad choices sometimes. We all take wrong actions. We all sin. It's been that way since Adam and Eve. But did you notice that even when Adam and Eve broke everything when they bit into that fruit, God still took care of them?

Bad consequences come from our bad choices. But what's most important is how we learn from our mistakes. What steps did we take to get into this mess? How can we avoid them next time? What does the Bible teach us about staying away from this sin? Who around us can help us create better habits?

Ask for God's forgiveness when you fall, and let Him pick you back up again. He loves you just as much and wants to help you grow. Making mistakes is only human. But not learning from them is being a dummy. Don't be a dummy. Be a human growing stronger in God.

YOUR MISSION

1. Assess yourself by making a list of your strengths and weaknesses. We've all got both.

2. Build a good habit. Choose an action or trait you want to improve. Pick one step you can take to help, and do it for thirty days. Examples might be acting more grateful by thanking your mom for dinner each night—or beating a temptation by memorizing a verse like 1 Corinthians 10:13 and saying it every day.

3. Draw a picture of what you think life would be like now if Adam and Eve hadn't sinned.

YOUR DEBRIEF

• What mistakes have you made recently?

• What have you learned from them?

• How can you avoid them next time?

MISSION ACCOMPLISHED

What did you learn?

What do you want to remember?

BIG PICTURE PAGE

WRITE DOWN SOME DREAMS YOU
HAVE FOR THE NEXT YEAR.

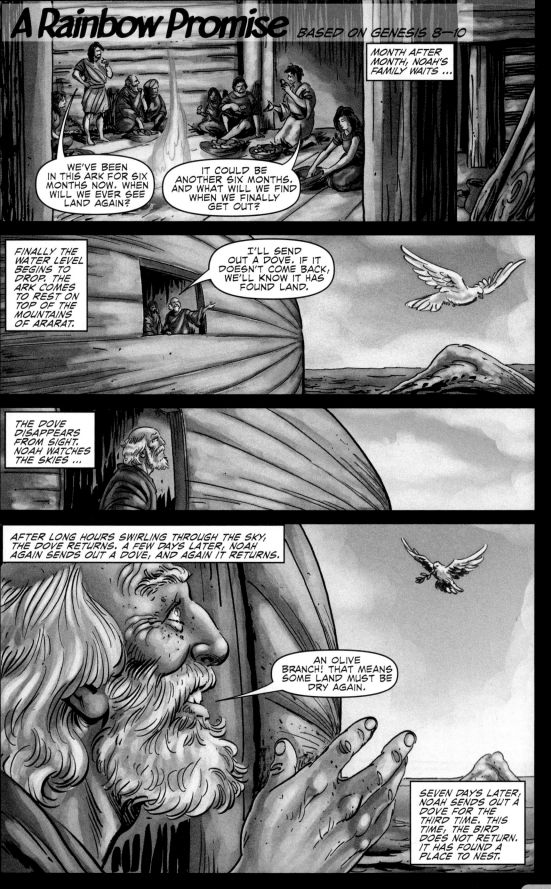

A Rainbow Promise
BASED ON GENESIS 8—10

MONTH AFTER MONTH, NOAH'S FAMILY WAITS ...

WE'VE BEEN IN THIS ARK FOR SIX MONTHS NOW. WHEN WILL WE EVER SEE LAND AGAIN?

IT COULD BE ANOTHER SIX MONTHS. AND WHAT WILL WE FIND WHEN WE FINALLY GET OUT?

FINALLY THE WATER LEVEL BEGINS TO DROP. THE ARK COMES TO REST ON TOP OF THE MOUNTAINS OF ARARAT.

I'LL SEND OUT A DOVE. IF IT DOESN'T COME BACK, WE'LL KNOW IT HAS FOUND LAND.

THE DOVE DISAPPEARS FROM SIGHT. NOAH WATCHES THE SKIES ...

AFTER LONG HOURS SWIRLING THROUGH THE SKY, THE DOVE RETURNS. A FEW DAYS LATER, NOAH AGAIN SENDS OUT A DOVE, AND AGAIN IT RETURNS.

AN OLIVE BRANCH! THAT MEANS SOME LAND MUST BE DRY AGAIN.

SEVEN DAYS LATER, NOAH SENDS OUT A DOVE FOR THE THIRD TIME. THIS TIME, THE BIRD DOES NOT RETURN. IT HAS FOUND A PLACE TO NEST.

NOAH AND HIS FAMILY ARE ANXIOUS TO LEAVE THE ARK. THEY LOOK EVERY DAY FOR SIGNS OF DRY LAND.

LOOK!

A LITTLE OVER A YEAR AFTER THE FLOOD STARTED, NOAH STEPS OUT ONTO DRY LAND ONCE MORE. ONLY EIGHT PEOPLE HAVE SURVIVED THE FLOOD: NOAH, HIS WIFE, THEIR THREE SONS, AND THEIR SONS' WIVES.

THE WARM SUN ON MY FACE, THE GRASS UNDER MY FEET—IT FEELS WONDERFUL!

EVERYTHING EVIL IS GONE. THROUGH US, GOD IS GIVING HUMAN BEINGS A NEW START. WE MUST OBEY GOD AND TEACH EVERYONE WHO FOLLOWS US TO OBEY.

OH, GROUND! HOW I'VE MISSED YOU!!

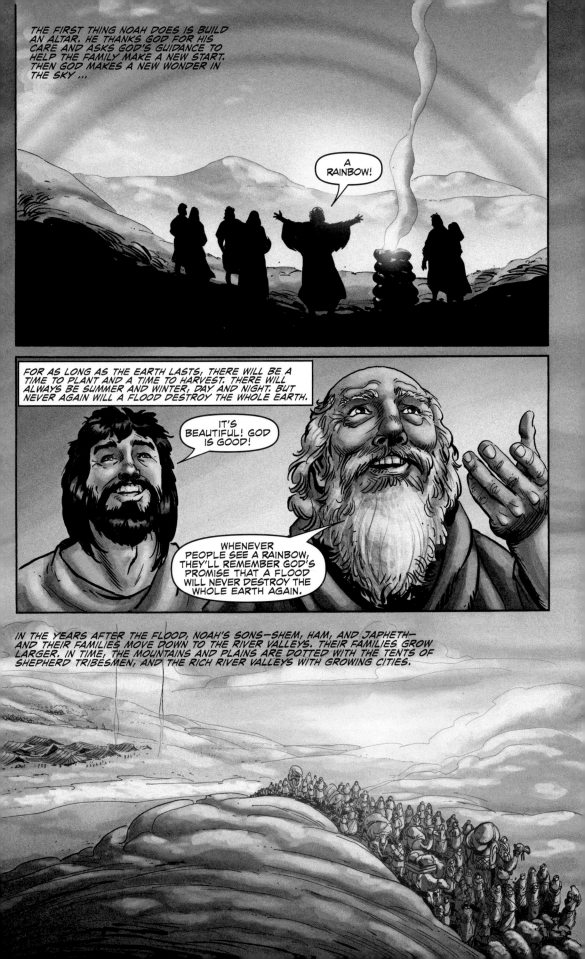

A RAINBOW PROMISE

KEY VERSE

WHEN I SEND CLOUDS OVER THE EARTH, THE RAINBOW WILL APPEAR IN THE CLOUDS, AND I WILL REMEMBER MY COVENANT WITH YOU AND WITH ALL LIVING CREATURES. NEVER AGAIN WILL THE FLOODWATERS DESTROY ALL LIFE.

—Genesis 9:14–15 NLT

X-RAY VISION

You think you'll remember it forever—the craziest roller-coaster ride, your best birthday ever, scoring the winning goal, winning a big award. At the time it feels bigger-than-anything-in-the-world-ever awesome. But then a month goes by, and a season, and a year. It's not that you totally forget. But other stuff happens. Your memory just sort of … fades.

You'd think Noah and his family would never forget something as crazy as the flood and floating around with all those animals. I'm sure they never forgot it completely. But life went on. Every new day put the flood farther into the past. Except when they saw a rainbow!

The rainbow was a reminder. It must have brought the memories flooding back to Noah and his family (get it, *flooding* back?): *Hey, Ham, remember how God took care of us during the flood?* It even reminded God! And it still reminds us today of His goodness.

We all need reminders. God later had His people set up rock towers to remind them of His miracles (check out "Entering the Promised Land" in *The Action Bible*). Now we have the Bible to remind us. But we can also make notes and symbols to jog our memories too—objects or items that help us go, *Oh yeah! That was so cool when God did that to help me. And if He took care of me then, He can do it again.* Start to remember the past, and build new courage for the future.

YOUR MISSION

1. Start a journal. Write down how God answers your prayers and helps you. Go back every so often to remember and get encouraged.

2. Rock a reminder. Start building a small tower in your yard. Write on flat rocks short reminders of good things God does and stack them. Hand-sized flat river rocks work best. Thank God whenever you see it.

3. Build Noah's ark. Use Legos, cardboard, wood, or any other supplies you have.

YOUR DEBRIEF

• What specific things make you think about God?

• What are your favorite memories?

• What things around you make you say, "Thanks, God. That was so cool!"?

MISSION ACCOMPLISHED

What did you learn?

What do you want to remember?

BIG PICTURE PAGE

USE YOUR FAMILY PHOTOS AND VIDEOS TO MAKE
A MOVIE OR SLIDE SHOW OF SOME FAVORITE
MEMORIES. USE THIS SPACE TO DRAW AND PLAN.

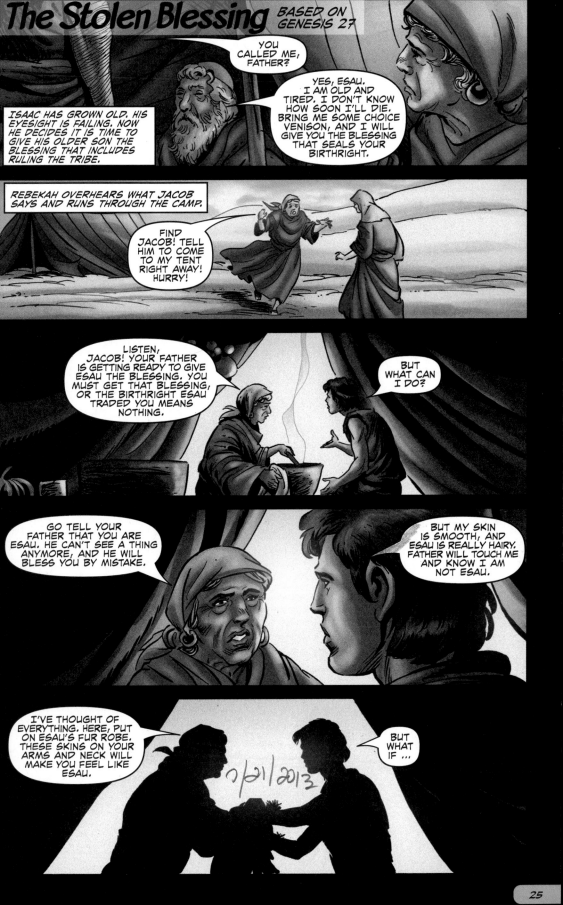

The Stolen Blessing
BASED ON GENESIS 27

YOU CALLED ME, FATHER?

YES, ESAU. I AM OLD AND TIRED. I DON'T KNOW HOW SOON I'LL DIE. BRING ME SOME CHOICE VENISON, AND I WILL GIVE YOU THE BLESSING THAT SEALS YOUR BIRTHRIGHT.

ISAAC HAS GROWN OLD. HIS EYESIGHT IS FAILING. NOW HE DECIDES IT IS TIME TO GIVE HIS OLDER SON THE BLESSING THAT INCLUDES RULING THE TRIBE.

REBEKAH OVERHEARS WHAT JACOB SAYS AND RUNS THROUGH THE CAMP.

FIND JACOB! TELL HIM TO COME TO MY TENT RIGHT AWAY! HURRY!

LISTEN, JACOB! YOUR FATHER IS GETTING READY TO GIVE ESAU THE BLESSING. YOU MUST GET THAT BLESSING, OR THE BIRTHRIGHT ESAU TRADED YOU MEANS NOTHING.

BUT WHAT CAN I DO?

GO TELL YOUR FATHER THAT YOU ARE ESAU. HE CAN'T SEE A THING ANYMORE, AND HE WILL BLESS YOU BY MISTAKE.

BUT MY SKIN IS SMOOTH, AND ESAU IS REALLY HAIRY. FATHER WILL TOUCH ME AND KNOW I AM NOT ESAU.

I'VE THOUGHT OF EVERYTHING. HERE, PUT ON ESAU'S FUR ROBE. THESE SKINS ON YOUR ARMS AND NECK WILL MAKE YOU FEEL LIKE ESAU.

BUT WHAT IF ...

IT'S STRANGE. THE VOICE SOUNDS LIKE JACOB, BUT THE HANDS ARE ESAU'S. ARE YOU REALLY ESAU?

YES, I AM.

WILL HE BELIEVE ME? . . .

HE DOES ...

GOD GIVE YOU THE RICHNESS OF THE EARTH. LET THE PEOPLE SERVE YOU, AND NATIONS BOW DOWN TO YOU. BE MASTER OVER YOUR BROTHERS. CURSED BE EVERYONE WHO CURSES YOU, AND BLESSED BE EVERYONE WHO BLESSES YOU.

NO SOONER HAS ISAAC GIVEN THE BLESSING THAN JACOB RUSHES OUT OF HIS FATHER'S TENT.

MOTHER! THE BLESSING IS MINE! BUT WHAT WILL ESAU DO?

NO MATTER WHAT ESAU DOES, THE BLESSING IS YOURS. NOT EVEN YOUR FATHER CAN TAKE IT BACK NOW.

BUT WHILE JACOB AND HIS MOTHER ARE REJOICING, ESAU RETURNS.

THE STOLEN BLESSING

KEY VERSE

ESAU EXCLAIMED, "NO WONDER HIS NAME IS JACOB, FOR NOW HE HAS CHEATED ME TWICE. FIRST HE TOOK MY RIGHTS AS THE FIRSTBORN, AND NOW HE HAS STOLEN MY BLESSING."

—Genesis 27:36 NLT

X-RAY VISION

Ah, brothers and sisters. Sometimes you love 'em. Sometimes you can't stand 'em. They can be your best friends one minute and your worst enemies the next. They're always crossing onto your side in the backseat of the car or playing with the toy you want. When you say "did not," they say "did too." When you say "uh-huh," they say "nuh-uh." It can seem like their main purpose in life is to drive you totally bonkers.

That's probably what Esau and Jacob thought about each other. Their rivalry got so bad that Jacob cheated Esau out of his inheritance and Esau plotted to kill Jacob. Not exactly brotherly love.

But would you believe your sisses and bros are a special gift to you? It might take a few years to realize it, but they can be some of your best friends forever. They share your life like no one else can. They'll always be there because they're your family. For now they can always give you somebody to play or hang with. For later they can have your back like nobody else can. Why not start making the most of a good relationship now?

YOUR MISSION

If you don't have any brothers or sisters, do these activities for a friend.

1. How do you bug your bro or sis the most? Don't do that all week.

2. Give your sibling a surprise gift.

3. Forgive a sib. Write down what you hate most about a brother or sister. Then rip it up and throw it away.

YOUR DEBRIEF

- What are the most fun times you've had with your brothers and sisters?

- What one thing can you do to help a sibling relationship?

- Do you need to talk to a parent about problems with a brother or sister?

MISSION ACCOMPLISHED

What did you learn?

What do you want to remember?

SHARE THE ADVENTURE

Make a photo book with pictures of you and your bros and sisses. Get your parents to help you print one professionally online.

BIG PICTURE PAGE

BE A PRO PHOTOGRAPHER THIS WEEK. STICK A FEW OF YOUR FAVORITE SHOTS HERE. BONUS IF YOU GIVE COPIES TO YOUR FAMILY MEMBERS.

Wife Swap BASED ON GENESIS 29

JACOB CONTINUES HIS JOURNEY. AT LAST HE GETS CLOSE TO HARAN.

MAYBE THOSE SHEPHERDS AT THE WELL CAN HELP ME FIND MY UNCLE LABAN.

CAN YOU TELL ME HOW TO FIND THE CHIEFTAIN, LABAN?

SURE! LABAN? THAT FLOCK OF SHEEP IS HIS. THAT'S HIS DAUGHTER RACHEL WITH THEM.

SHE'S GORGEOUS!

QUICKLY JACOB ROLLS THE STONE FROM THE WELL AND HELPS RACHEL WATER THE SHEEP. WHEN HE TELLS HER WHO HE IS, SHE RUNS TO FIND HER FATHER.

THAT NIGHT, LABAN HOLDS A FEAST FOR HIS NEPHEW JACOB. LEAH, THE OLDER DAUGHTER, SERVES THE FOOD, WHILE RACHEL, THE YOUNGER DAUGHTER, LISTENS TO JACOB TELL ABOUT HIS HOME AND THE LONG JOURNEY TO HARAN.

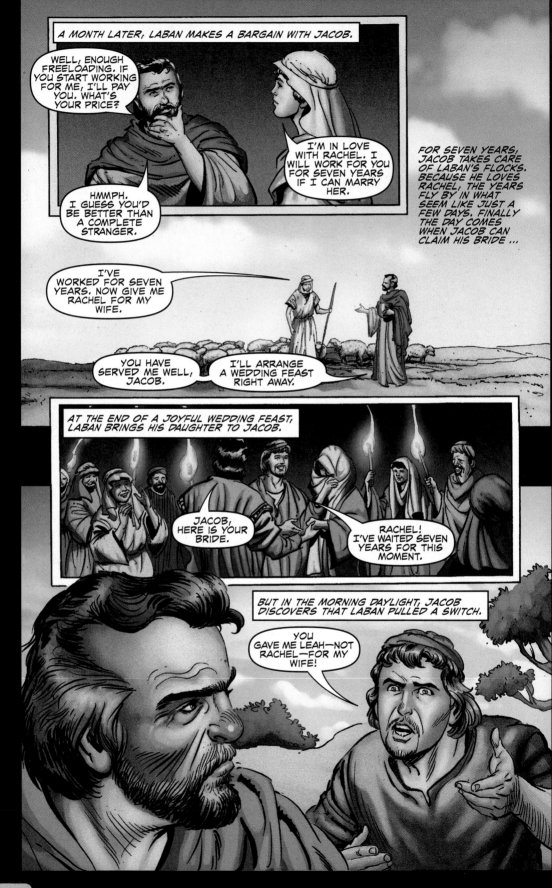

A MONTH LATER, LABAN MAKES A BARGAIN WITH JACOB.

WELL, ENOUGH FREELOADING. IF YOU START WORKING FOR ME, I'LL PAY YOU. WHAT'S YOUR PRICE?

I'M IN LOVE WITH RACHEL. I WILL WORK FOR YOU FOR SEVEN YEARS IF I CAN MARRY HER.

HMMPH. I GUESS YOU'D BE BETTER THAN A COMPLETE STRANGER.

FOR SEVEN YEARS, JACOB TAKES CARE OF LABAN'S FLOCKS. BECAUSE HE LOVES RACHEL, THE YEARS FLY BY IN WHAT SEEM LIKE JUST A FEW DAYS. FINALLY THE DAY COMES WHEN JACOB CAN CLAIM HIS BRIDE ...

I'VE WORKED FOR SEVEN YEARS. NOW GIVE ME RACHEL FOR MY WIFE.

YOU HAVE SERVED ME WELL, JACOB.

I'LL ARRANGE A WEDDING FEAST RIGHT AWAY.

AT THE END OF A JOYFUL WEDDING FEAST, LABAN BRINGS HIS DAUGHTER TO JACOB.

JACOB, HERE IS YOUR BRIDE.

RACHEL! I'VE WAITED SEVEN YEARS FOR THIS MOMENT.

BUT IN THE MORNING DAYLIGHT, JACOB DISCOVERS THAT LABAN PULLED A SWITCH.

YOU GAVE ME LEAH—NOT RACHEL—FOR MY WIFE!

KEY VERSE

BUT WHEN JACOB WOKE UP IN THE MORNING—IT WAS LEAH! "WHAT HAVE YOU DONE TO ME?" JACOB RAGED AT LABAN. "I WORKED SEVEN YEARS FOR RACHEL! WHY HAVE YOU TRICKED ME?"

—Genesis 29:25 NLT

X-RAY VISION

Did Jacob get cheated or what?! The guy works for seven years—seven years! That's most of your life! He thinks he's getting the wife of his dreams, Rachel. Then the day after the wedding he gazes into his new bride's eyes and discovers he's been tricked! BIG bummer!

This kind of trick would be nearly impossible in our culture today, but back in Bible times it was easy to pull off. Still, this story makes us want to cry foul. But think back a few Bible stories. Jacob was a master trickster. He spent many years conning his brother and stealing the family inheritance from his father. You might say he finally got a taste of his own medicine from Laban.

You've heard the sayings: *What goes around comes around. You reap what you sow. You get what you deserve.* They don't make Laban's trick right. But they remind us of a powerful life truth: every action has a consequence. Keep lying and cheating people, and it will eventually come back to haunt you. In Jacob's case, he finally got cheated in a big way.

The good news is the equation works both ways. Good actions bring good consequences. Treat people with generosity and kindness, and you'll probably get back more of the same. Learn from Jacob's mistakes; don't make your own. Want good consequences? Choose good actions.

YOUR MISSION

1. Make a list of unexpected, surprise acts of kindness you can do for others. Now do one every day this week—and watch how people respond.

2. Talk to a friend or family member you've been fighting with. Apologize and forgive.

3. Draw a consequence map. Write down decisions you often make, good and bad; then follow where those actions lead you. Start with talking back to your parents, calling a friend a name, or telling a lie.

YOUR DEBRIEF

- If Jacob made such bad choices, why did God choose to use him?

- How do we know Jacob learned from his actions? For a hint, read "Touched by an Angel" in *The Action Bible*.

- What kind of actions and choices do you need to change to find better consequences in your life?

MISSION ACCOMPLISHED

What did you learn?

What do you want to remember?

Jailhouse Shock

FALSELY ACCUSED, JOSEPH FACES HIS FIRST NIGHT IN PRISON. BUT HE IS NOT AFRAID, AND HE IS NOT ALONE, BECAUSE GOD IS WITH HIM. JOSEPH PRAYS JUST AS HE HAS DONE EVERY OTHER NIGHT OF HIS LIFE.

WHAT GOD CAN SAVE HIM?

LEAVE HIM ALONE! HE'S BRAVER THAN THE REST OF US.

ONE LONG, HOT DAY FOLLOWS ANOTHER. THE PRISONERS QUARREL OVER FOOD, WATER, AND THE BEST PLACE TO SLEEP. ONE DAY A FIGHT BREAKS OUT ...

STOP IT! FIGHTING WON'T MAKE LIFE ANY BETTER.

EVEN IN PRISON, GOD IS WITH JOSEPH. THROUGH THESE TRIALS, GOD IS FORCING JOSEPH TO LEARN PATIENCE AND LEADERSHIP. WHEN THE KEEPER OF THE JAIL DISCOVERS THAT JOSEPH MAINTAINS PEACE IN THE PRISON, HE PUTS JOSEPH IN CHARGE OF THE OTHER PRISONERS.

ONE DAY, THE KING'S BAKER AND BUTLER ARE THROWN INTO PRISON FOR OFFENDING THE KING. BOTH MEN HAVE DREAMS THAT DISTURB THEM AND COME TO JOSEPH FOR HELP.

WHAT DO YOU THINK MY DREAM MEANS?

NOW TELL ME WHAT MY DREAM MEANS. LIKE HIS WOULD BE NICE!

I'M VERY SORRY. YOUR DREAM SHOWS THAT IN THREE DAYS YOUR HEAD WILL BE LIFTED OFF—YOU WILL BE HANGED UP HIGH BY PHARAOH.

IN THREE DAYS, YOUR HEAD WILL BE LIFTED UP, AND PHARAOH WILL GIVE YOU BACK YOUR HIGH POSITION. YOU WILL BE THE KING'S BUTLER AGAIN. AND PLEASE, WHEN MY WORDS COME TRUE, ASK PHARAOH TO RELEASE ME FROM PRISON. I AM AN INNOCENT CAPTIVE.

JOSEPH'S WORDS COME TRUE. THREE DAYS LATER, ONE MAN IS EXECUTED AND THE OTHER RETURNS TO SERVE THE KING. BUT THE BUTLER FORGETS HIS PROMISE TO PUT IN A GOOD WORD FOR JOSEPH. TWO YEARS GO BY. ONE DAY PHARAOH SUMMONS HIS BUTLER.

NO WINE FOR ME TODAY. I HAVE HAD A DISTURBING DREAM, AND NO ONE IN MY WHOLE KINGDOM CAN TELL ME WHAT IT MEANS.

PHARAOH, I KNOW OF A HEBREW PRISONER WHO CAN TELL THE MEANING OF DREAMS. HE EXPLAINED MINE!

WELL, WHAT ARE YOU WAITING FOR?!

JAILHOUSE SHOCK

KEY VERSE

BUT THE Lord WAS WITH JOSEPH IN THE PRISON AND SHOWED HIM HIS FAITHFUL LOVE. AND THE Lord MADE JOSEPH A FAVORITE WITH THE PRISON WARDEN.

—Genesis 39:21 NLT

X-RAY VISION

Your sister gets some new clothes, and you don't. *That's not fair!* Your brother gets more doughnuts than you. *That's not fair!* Your friend's class doesn't have to take the test. *That's not fair!* Your team has to play the state champions in the tournament. Say it with me now one more time—*That's not fair!*

Joseph had good reason to join in the chant. Get this: his brothers beat him up, threw him in a pit, then sold him as a slave! *That's not fair!* Things started looking up when he was put in charge of his Egyptian master's house. But then when he did the right thing, the master's wife falsely accused him, and he got sent to jail. *That's not fair!* Then he helped the other prisoners and still had to wait a couple years until they remembered to help him. *That's not fair!*

I hate to break this to you, but … life's not fair. Yes, you've heard it from your parents, too, but it's really true. It's the reality of living in a broken world. Sometimes things go your way; sometimes they don't. But what's also true is that God is always good. He's got a much bigger view, and He's able to work good even in bad situations. Take it from Joseph. Quit worrying about what's fair or not. Practice looking for God's good no matter what's going on.

YOUR MISSION

1. Pay your parents a dollar every time you say "That's not fair" this week.

2. For every situation you *want* to say "That's not fair," write down ideas of how you might see God's goodness.

3. Memorize Genesis 50:20.

YOUR DEBRIEF

- Why do we call "unfair" only when a situation goes against us?

- What gifts and opportunities do you have that are different from your brothers' and sisters' (or your friends')?

- What can you do if you're wrongly accused?

MISSION ACCOMPLISHED

What did you learn?

What do you want to remember?

BIG PICTURE PAGE

DRAW A SELF-PORTRAIT.

Baby in a Basket

BASED ON EXODUS 1:1–2:10

THERE ARE TOO MANY HEBREWS IN EGYPT! IF WE HAD A WAR, THEY MIGHT TURN AGAINST US. I MUST FIND A WAY TO KEEP THEM FROM CAUSING TROUBLE.

THE NEW PHARAOH IN EGYPT HAS FORGOTTEN THAT THE HEBREWS' ANCESTOR JOSEPH SAVED EGYPT FROM THE FAMINE. FROM HIS ROYAL YACHT ON THE NILE, THE KING FROWNS AS HE WATCHES THE HEBREW SHEPHERDS WITH THEIR RICH FLOCKS.

THE NEXT DAY, THE KING INSPECTS A NEW BUILDING PROJECT.

WE NEED THOUSANDS MORE WORKERS TO GET THIS JOB DONE.

THIS SOUNDS LIKE A PERFECT JOB FOR THE HEBREWS. THEY WILL WORK AS SLAVES. IT WILL SAVE US MONEY; AND THEN THOSE FOREIGNERS WON'T BE ABLE TO CAUSE TROUBLE.

SO FROM DAYLIGHT TO DARK, HEBREW MEN AND BOYS ARE DRIVEN FROM THEIR HOMES AND FORCED TO WORK UNDER WHIP-CRACKING SLAVE DRIVERS.

BUT WITH GOD'S BLESSING, THE HEBREWS FLOURISH AND GROW STRONGER—EVEN UNDER THE HARSH CONDITIONS!

WE WORK THEM HARDER EVERY DAY, BUT THERE ARE MORE HEBREWS THAN BEFORE. THE KING WILL NOT BE HAPPY ABOUT THIS ...

WHEN PHARAOH HEARS THE REPORT ...

I'LL TAKE CARE OF THE SLAVES! THROW EVERY HEBREW BOY BABY INTO THE NILE RIVER!

THE CRUEL ORDER IS CARRIED OUT. HEBREW MOTHERS AND FATHERS RISK THEIR LIVES TO PROTECT THEIR SONS, BUT THE KING'S MEN NEVER GIVE UP ON THEIR SEARCH.

NIGHT AFTER NIGHT, AMRAM, A HEBREW FROM THE TRIBE OF LEVI, HURRIES HOME FROM WORK—AFRAID THAT THE SOLDIERS HAVE VISITED HIS HOME.

O GOD, HELP US KEEP OUR NEW BABY BOY SAFE FROM THE EGYPTIANS.

THE MAID BRINGS THE BASKET TO THE PRINCESS, WHO OPENS IT.

A HEBREW BABY! LISTEN TO HIM CRY! WE HAVE TO FIND SOMEONE TO FEED AND CARE FOR HIM.

JUST THEN, MIRIAM STEPS OUT OF THE BUSHES.

SHALL I FIND A HEBREW NURSE FOR THE BABY?

YES. BRING ONE TO ME AS SOON AS YOU CAN.

MOTHER! COME RIGHT AWAY. THE PRINCESS HAS FOUND OUR BABY—AND SHE WANTS A HEBREW NURSE TO TAKE CARE OF HIM.

GOD HAS ANSWERED MY PRAYER, MIRIAM. MY SON WILL BE SAFE WITH THE PRINCESS.

AT THE RIVER'S EDGE ...

TAKE THIS BABY AND CARE FOR HIM. IF ANYONE QUESTIONS YOU, SEND WORD TO ME AT ONCE. I'M NAMING HIM MOSES, BECAUSE I PULLED HIM OUT OF THE WATER.

BABY IN A BASKET

KEY VERSE

THE WOMAN BECAME PREGNANT AND GAVE BIRTH TO A SON. SHE SAW THAT HE WAS A SPECIAL BABY AND KEPT HIM HIDDEN FOR THREE MONTHS.

—Exodus 2:2 NLT

X-RAY VISION

Let's say an evil ruler took over the country and ordered soldiers to kill every new baby who was born. Way harsh! Now let's say your mom was pregnant and had a baby—you. Way cool! But remember that law? So she hides you, dodging soldiers and keeping you quiet for three whole months. Way heroic! She risks her own life to make sure you keep yours.

That's exactly what Moses's mom did. It worked until there were too many close calls. Her baby was getting bigger and louder, and the soldiers were closing in. So she came up with another plan to save her baby's life.

Your mom would probably do the same. Don't think she's got heroic stuff? You'd be surprised. Put a kid on the line, and a nice mom turns as fierce as a mama grizzly bear. Even more, the things your mom does every day for you and your family are pretty heroic. Think about it: sacrifice, service, strength. Do you think she always *feels* like coming to your rescue with homework help or a lost lunch box? Probably not, but she'll do it again and again because she loves you with an incredibly deep mom-love.

So show your mom you care. Let her know you notice. Say thank you. Help her out. Give her a break. Listen to and do what she says. Don't talk back. Do your chores without being asked and without complaining. Your mom makes your day all the time whether you realize it or not. It's time you made hers, too.

YOUR MISSION

1. Don't wait for Mother's Day. Make your mom a note or card now to show your appreciation.

2. Cook dinner for your family one night this week.

3. Make something to help your mom: maybe a key hanger or a homemade calendar.

YOUR DEBRIEF

• How can you show appreciation and love for your mom more often?

• What do you love most about your mom?

• What's one thing you can do to improve your relationship with your mom?

MISSION ACCOMPLISHED

What did you learn?

What do you want to remember?

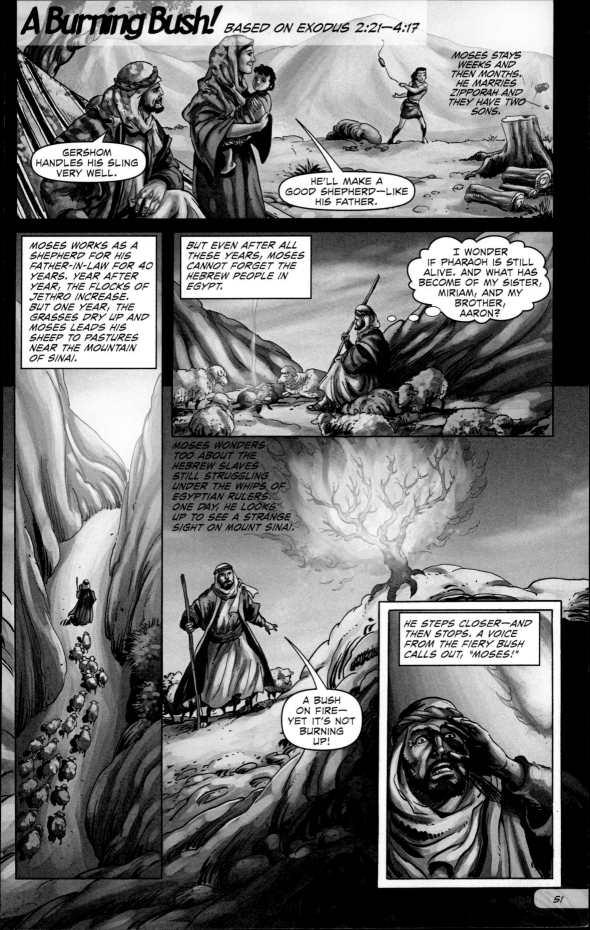

A Burning Bush!

BASED ON EXODUS 2:21–4:17

MOSES STAYS WEEKS AND THEN MONTHS. HE MARRIES ZIPPORAH AND THEY HAVE TWO SONS.

GERSHOM HANDLES HIS SLING VERY WELL.

HE'LL MAKE A GOOD SHEPHERD—LIKE HIS FATHER.

MOSES WORKS AS A SHEPHERD FOR HIS FATHER-IN-LAW FOR 40 YEARS. YEAR AFTER YEAR, THE FLOCKS OF JETHRO INCREASE. BUT ONE YEAR, THE GRASSES DRY UP AND MOSES LEADS HIS SHEEP TO PASTURES NEAR THE MOUNTAIN OF SINAI.

BUT EVEN AFTER ALL THESE YEARS, MOSES CANNOT FORGET THE HEBREW PEOPLE IN EGYPT.

I WONDER IF PHARAOH IS STILL ALIVE. AND WHAT HAS BECOME OF MY SISTER, MIRIAM, AND MY BROTHER, AARON?

MOSES WONDERS TOO ABOUT THE HEBREW SLAVES STILL STRUGGLING UNDER THE WHIPS OF EGYPTIAN RULERS. ONE DAY, HE LOOKS UP TO SEE A STRANGE SIGHT ON MOUNT SINAI.

A BUSH ON FIRE— YET IT'S NOT BURNING UP!

HE STEPS CLOSER—AND THEN STOPS. A VOICE FROM THE FIERY BUSH CALLS OUT, "MOSES!"

A BURNING BUSH!

KEY VERSE

NOW GO; I WILL HELP YOU SPEAK AND WILL TEACH YOU WHAT TO SAY.

—Exodus 4:12 NIV

X-RAY VISION

It's the last thing on earth you want to do. You know the dread. Each shoe feels like two tons as you plod toward your fate. You'd give a million dollars— or even your entire collection of pressed pennies—to get out of having to do *this* (whatever thing it is you don't want to do).

That's how Moses must have felt. Egypt was the last place he wanted to go. He'd spent forty years hiding out from the land of pyramids. He'd built a whole new life and family. He thought he had escaped his past in Egypt. Then out of the blue God showed up in that burning bush. Moses gave his best excuses, but his weaknesses didn't matter. God knew His own strength. It was time for Moses to face his fears.

The time comes for us to face our fears too. What are yours? The best thing Moses had going for him was God's help. God promised to give him everything he needed: miracles, the right words, and even his brother to help him. Moses just had to go and do what God showed him. It works the same for you. God is way bigger than your fears, and He's promised to always be with you. What are you waiting for?

YOUR MISSION

1. Sculpt a creature out of clay to represent your fears. Pick up a rock—that shows God's strength—and smash that fear-creature flat as a pancake.

2. Make yourself a necklace or bracelet to remind you that God is with you—always.

3. List three things you've been afraid of doing. Then do at least one this week.

YOUR DEBRIEF

- What have your parents been encouraging you to try?

- Have you ever felt like God has been calling you to do something, but you've been afraid? What is it?

- What have you dreamed about but been scared to go for?

MISSION ACCOMPLISHED

What did you learn?

What do you want to remember?

SHARE THE ADVENTURE

Do you have fears that make you actually sick? Do they give you panic attacks? Talk with your parents about them and get their help.

The Complaining Begins

BASED ON EXODUS 15:22–17:7

FROM THE RED SEA, THE ISRAELITES MARCH ACROSS THE DESERT. BUT AFTER DAYS OF TRAVEL THEY FORGET WHAT GOD HAS DONE FOR THEM. AND THEY BEGIN TO COMPLAIN ...

I'M THIRSTY.

THREE DAYS AND NO WATER IN SIGHT!

AT LAST THEY FIND A SPRING, BUT ...

IT'S BITTER! WE CAN'T DRINK THIS!

WE'LL ALL DIE OF THIRST.

THE PEOPLE COMPLAIN TO MOSES WHILE HE IS SITTING AS A JUDGE. MOSES PRAYS TO GOD FOR HELP—AND GOD POINTS OUT A NEARBY BRANCH. MOSES THROWS IT INTO THE SPRING.

NOW TASTE THE WATER AND KNOW THE POWER OF GOD!

IT'S CLEAN NOW.

GOD HAS SAVED US AGAIN. NOW I *KNOW* GOD IS GUIDING MOSES.

THE PEOPLE CONTINUE THEIR JOURNEY. AS THEY TRAVEL ACROSS THE HOT SANDS, THEIR THOUGHTS ARE OF THE HOMELAND GOD PROMISED THEM. THEY DREAM OF GREEN FIELDS ... FRESH STREAMS ... GREAT FLOCKS. BUT THEN THERE IS NO FOOD IN THE DESERT. THE PEOPLE GROW HUNGRY. THEY FORGET THAT GOD CARED FOR THEM WHEN THEY WERE THIRSTY. ANGRILY, THEY GO TO MOSES AND AARON.

LOOK— OUR FOOD IS GONE. HOW CAN WE FEED OUR CHILDREN?

THE LORD SHOULD HAVE JUST KILLED US IN EGYPT. THERE WE HAD POTS FULL OF MEAT! MMMM. ALL THE MEAT WE COULD EAT!

HAVE YOU BROUGHT US OUT HERE IN THE WILDERNESS TO STARVE US TO DEATH?

I AM SICK OF YOUR GRUMBLING! THIS EVENING, COME BEFORE THE LORD, AND HE WILL SHOW YOU HIS MIGHT!

BUT THE NEXT MORNING ...

UGH! IT'S SPOILED!

MOSES WARNED US. WE HAVE TO HAVE FAITH THAT GOD WILL TAKE CARE OF US.

ON THE SIXTH DAY OF THE WEEK, THE PEOPLE GATHER FOOD FOR THAT DAY AND THE SABBATH. THE FOOD KEPT FOR THE SABBATH DOES NOT SPOIL, AND NO NEW MANNA APPEARS ON THE GROUND.

WITH RENEWED FAITH IN GOD, THE ISRAELITES CONTINUE THEIR JOURNEY. THEY TRAVEL TOWARD MOUNT SINAI, WHERE MOSES WAS CALLED BY GOD TO SET THEM FREE FROM SLAVERY. MOSES SENDS HIS WIFE AND TWO SONS ON AHEAD TO VISIT THEIR OLD HOME.

TELL YOUR FATHER, JETHRO, WHAT GOD HAS DONE FOR OUR PEOPLE.

FARTHER ON ... WHILE THE ISRAELITES CAMP IN A PEACEFUL VALLEY, FIERCE TRIBESMEN WATCH FROM THE HILLS ...

THIS WILL BE EASY— A SURPRISE ATTACK, AND THE CAMP IS OURS!

THE COMPLAINING BEGINS

KEY VERSE

THERE, TOO, THE WHOLE COMMUNITY OF ISRAEL COMPLAINED ABOUT MOSES AND AARON. "IF ONLY THE LORD HAD KILLED US BACK IN EGYPT," THEY MOANED. "THERE WE SAT AROUND POTS FILLED WITH MEAT AND ATE ALL THE BREAD WE WANTED. BUT NOW YOU HAVE BROUGHT US INTO THIS WILDERNESS TO STARVE US ALL TO DEATH."

—Exodus 16:2–3 NLT

X-RAY VISION

Complaining is like mold. Ever watch mold grow? It starts with a little spot of white or black fungus. Then before you know it, your old bread is covered in polka dots of hairy fuzz. It's ruined. *Blech!*

All it takes is one complainer to spread a "bad attitude fungus" through your whole class, team, or family. Suddenly a good time—or the chance to turn a bummer into a bonus—goes straight into the trash can. Complaining often starts with forgetting: forgetting that things aren't really as bad as they seem, forgetting that your positive attitude is the first step toward fun, or forgetting how God has helped you in the past.

That's what happened to the Israelites. They watched God do amazing miracles to rescue them from the Egyptians, including parting the Red Sea. But three hard days later, they were wishing they were slaves again. Already they had turned their backs on Moses and God. A little complaining quickly turned into a moldy fungus that infected thousands. Of course, God came through with miraculous food and water, and the Israelites swore they'd never complain again. (Yeah, right.)

Don't be like the moldy Israelites. Cut off the complaining and spread positive words of hope instead. You can choose to stay positive.

YOUR MISSION

1. Remember. List three to ten great things about your life. These are reasons to be thankful.

2. Jog your memory. When you catch yourself starting to complain, pull out your paper as a reminder of all you have to stay positive about.

3. Pay up. Do ten push-ups or sit-ups every time you complain this week.

YOUR DEBRIEF

- What do you complain about most?

- Are there any situations or people you need to avoid to help you keep a better attitude?

- How can you spread yummy positive words instead of moldy negative complaints?

MISSION ACCOMPLISHED

What did you learn?

What do you want to remember?

"ARMED" BATTLE

KEY VERSE

LATER, WHEN MOSES' ARMS BECAME TIRED, THE MEN PUT A LARGE ROCK UNDER HIM, AND HE SAT ON IT. THEN AARON AND HUR HELD UP MOSES' HANDS—AARON ON ONE SIDE AND HUR ON THE OTHER. THEY KEPT HIS HANDS STEADY UNTIL THE SUN WENT DOWN.

—Exodus 17:12 NCV

X-RAY VISION

You can't seesaw by yourself. You can't take every shot. You can't play every instrument. You can't outdribble the entire defense. You can't carry on a conversation alone. You can't tickle yourself (go ahead, try it). You can't win all your battles on your own.

Neither could Joshua and his army or their leader, Moses. They all needed each other, and they all needed God. As long as Moses held his hands up to God, the Israelites were winning. But let them down, and they started losing. Have you ever tried holding your arms up all day long? It's impossible. But Moses had good friends who propped him and his arms up.

There's an old saying: No one is an island. It means none of us can survive alone in the middle of life's currents. We all need someone. We need friends to stick by us and make us stronger. Moses couldn't stand alone. Neither can you. Start *getting* good friends by *being* a good friend. Treat other people the way you want to be treated. You'll find you've got buddies willing to help prop you up when things get tough.

YOUR MISSION

1. Do an experiment. Hold up your arms as long as you can, and time it. See how much longer you can go with friends holding up your arms.

2. List what you like or want in a friend.

3. Practice doing that list for other people all week.

YOUR DEBRIEF

- Who is always there to stand by you?

- Is there anyone you need to apologize to?

- What have you been resisting help with?

MISSION ACCOMPLISHED

What did you learn?

What do you want to remember?

SHARE THE ADVENTURE

Start a lunch club. You and your friends invite people to eat with you at school. Don't let anyone eat alone.

BIG PICTURE PAGE

DRAW A COMIC STRIP OF A STORY THAT
SHOWS HOW A GOOD FRIEND ACTS.

A Golden Calf
BASED ON EXODUS 32

GOD GIVES MOSES MORE LAWS, AND WHEN THESE ARE WRITTEN DOWN, MOSES BUILDS AN ALTAR. HE AND HIS PEOPLE MAKE AN AGREEMENT, OR "COVENANT," WITH GOD. THE PEOPLE PROMISE TO FOLLOW ALL OF THE LORD'S COMMANDS.

LATER, GOD CALLS MOSES TO COME AGAIN TO MOUNT SINAI, WHERE HE WILL GIVE MOSES THE LAW WRITTEN ON STONE TABLETS. JOSHUA GOES PARTWAY WITH HIM. DAYS PASS, AND MOSES DOES NOT RETURN.

WHEN IS MOSES COMING BACK?

CAN WE GO LOOK FOR HIM?

WE DON'T KNOW WHEN MOSES WILL BE BACK. BUT YOU MUST NOT FOLLOW HIM UP THE MOUNTAIN. HE IS ALONE WITH GOD.

WHO KNOWS, MAYBE MOSES ISN'T COMING BACK ...

IF HE DOESN'T COME BACK, WHAT WILL WE DO?

LET'S ASK AARON TO LET US MAKE A STATUE TO WORSHIP.

YES! WE WANT A GOD WE CAN SEE.

FEELING LOST WITHOUT THEIR LEADER, THE PEOPLE FORGET GOD'S COMMANDMENTS AND THEIR PROMISE TO WORSHIP ONLY GOD. THEY BRING THEIR JEWELRY TO AARON, WHO MELTS IT AND MAKES A GOLDEN STATUE OF A CALF.

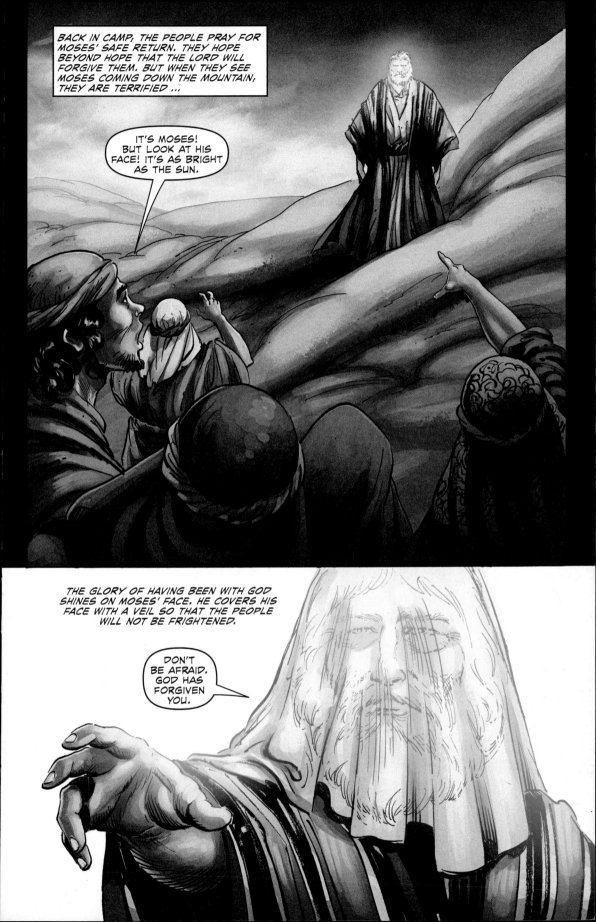

KEY VERSE

WHEN THE PEOPLE SAW HOW LONG IT WAS TAKING MOSES TO COME BACK DOWN THE MOUNTAIN, THEY GATHERED AROUND AARON. "COME ON," THEY SAID, "MAKE US SOME GODS WHO CAN LEAD US. WE DON'T KNOW WHAT HAPPENED TO THIS FELLOW MOSES, WHO BROUGHT US HERE FROM THE LAND OF EGYPT."

—Exodus 32:1 NLT

X-RAY VISION

"I'll believe it when I see it." Have you ever said that? Lots of times it's just easier to trust what we can look at with our own eyes. Maybe you feel that way about God—like it'd be easier to do what He wants if He'd just show up in front of you.

That's what the Israelites seemed to think. So they built themselves a big golden cow to worship. *Seriously?* Yep. They had seen the Egyptians worship statues, so they wanted one of their own as god. Never mind all the spectacular miracles they'd been seeing God do ever since they left Egypt. They wanted a party with a god they could see, even if it was a cow.

It's easy to laugh at the Israelites. I mean, how stupid can you get? But what about us? How often do we trust things we can see more than we trust God? Don't we follow fun and friends and money sometimes more than we follow God? Maybe that's because we can see them all around us. But our faith gets stronger when we trust that God's ways are best even when they're hard to see. Our spirits grow when we believe God will take care of us. And the more we watch the signs of God working around us, the easier it becomes to see Him.

YOUR MISSION

1. Look for God all around you. Make a list of the good things He does in your life.

2. Tear down an idol. Give up something that pulls you away from God. Maybe it's a friend, game, TV show, or hobby.

3. Confess a wrong to God. Write it on a paper with an apology to God. Shred it, and know it's gone because God forgives you.

YOUR DEBRIEF

- How is God like the wind?

- What other things do you follow instead of God?

- What is something you've looked back on and thought, *What was I thinking?*

MISSION ACCOMPLISHED

What did you learn?

What do you want to remember?

BIG PICTURE PAGE

NOW IT'S TIME TO ...

Spy vs. Spy
BASED ON NUMBERS 13:1–14:10

Mediterranean Sea

THE ISRAELITES CONTINUE THEIR JOURNEY UNTIL THEY REACH THE WILDERNESS OF PARAN. THERE MOSES ORDERS THEM TO SET UP CAMP.

CANAAN

Sea of Galilee

Wilderness of Paran

EGYPT

Camp
Mt. Sinai

Jordan River

Dead Sea

Red Sea

Arabian Desert

MIDIAN

MOSES CALLS ONE MAN FROM EACH TRIBE TO ATTEND AN IMPORTANT MEETING.

WE ARE ON THE BORDER OF CANAAN, THE LAND GOD HAS PROMISED TO US.

BUT BEFORE WE GO INTO IT, WE MUST KNOW WHAT LIES AHEAD.

WHAT ARE YOUR PLANS?

WE NEED TO EXPLORE THE LAND, JOSHUA.

WE MUST FIND OUT WHAT THE PEOPLE ARE LIKE, HOW MANY RIVERS WE WILL HAVE TO CROSS, HOW WELL THE CITIES ARE FORTIFIED.

IT'S A DANGEROUS JOB, BUT IT MUST BE DONE.

EACH MAN HERE CAN ACT AS A SCOUT, AND WE'LL GET STARTED RIGHT AWAY.

LOOK AT THAT CITY!

AND THE SIZE OF THOSE WALLS!

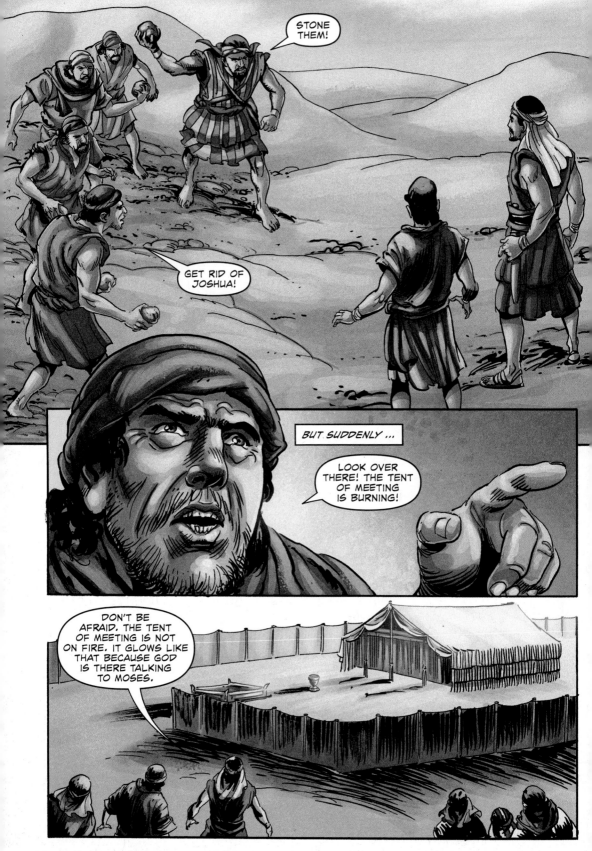

KEY VERSE

AND IF THE LORD IS PLEASED WITH US, HE WILL BRING US SAFELY INTO THAT LAND AND GIVE IT TO US. IT IS A RICH LAND FLOWING WITH MILK AND HONEY. DO NOT REBEL AGAINST THE LORD, AND DON'T BE AFRAID OF THE PEOPLE OF THE LAND. THEY ARE ONLY HELPLESS PREY TO US! THEY HAVE NO PROTECTION, BUT THE LORD IS WITH US! DON'T BE AFRAID OF THEM!

—Numbers 14:8–9 NLT

X-RAY VISION

You know how it is when you're riding a bike. Look too long at that bush or rock you're scared of hitting, and it's like a magnet. You smack right into it. But look ahead where you want to go, and you cruise right past.

Sounds like those ten other spies were staring too hard at the obstacles. Joshua and Caleb were looking straight ahead. It took real guts to stand up to the other ten spies. Then they stood up to millions of Israelites. And they were ready to stand up to any enemies they found in Canaan.

So why did Joshua and Caleb see things so differently from the other spies? What made them so brave when the entire nation was against them? Their courage came from looking at God. They were leaders because they concentrated on what God could do instead of what could go wrong. They knew what God had promised. They knew He had rescued them before. And they knew God would help them all the way to the end.

What are you afraid of? What are you giving in to the crowd about? What are you looking at—your fears and problems or God? Take courage by concentrating on all God can do.

YOUR MISSION

1. List your fears. Then write beside them how God can fix those situations.

2. Write a play including yourself in Joshua and Caleb's story and setting it in modern times.

3. Carry a coin in your pocket. When you're tempted to get worried or scared, flip the coin over as a reminder to look at the bright side and all that God can do to help you.

YOUR DEBRIEF

- When have you given in to the crowd?

- When have you stood strong for what you know is right?

- What do you need to take a stand for?

MISSION ACCOMPLISHED

What did you learn?

What do you want to remember?

IF I WERE AN EXPLORER, I WOULD ...

IN THE PROMISED LAND THE ISRAELITES FIND FRUIT AND GRAIN.

LOOK! FOOD ENOUGH FOR EVERYONE!

THANK GOD! THIS IS A WONDERFUL PLACE.

NOW THAT THE PEOPLE CAN FIND FOOD FOR THEMSELVES, GOD NO LONGER SENDS THE MANNA HE HAS SENT FOR 40 YEARS.

The Walls of Jericho
BASED ON JOSHUA 5-6

WHILE THE REST OF THE CAMP ENJOYS THE NEW LAND, JOSHUA SCOUTS THE AREA IN PREPARATION FOR THE ATTACK ON JERICHO. SUDDENLY HE LOOKS UP AND SEES A MAN WITH A SWORD!

IS HE GOING TO TRY TO KILL ME?

BUT JOSHUA IS NO COWARD. BRAVELY, HE FACES THE STRANGER.

ARE YOU FRIEND OR ENEMY?

NEITHER. I AM THE CAPTAIN OF THE LORD'S ARMY!

THE WALLS OF JERICHO

KEY VERSE

BUT THE Lord SAID TO JOSHUA, "I HAVE GIVEN YOU JERICHO, ITS KING, AND ALL ITS STRONG WARRIORS. YOU AND YOUR FIGHTING MEN SHOULD MARCH AROUND THE TOWN ONCE A DAY FOR SIX DAYS.

—Joshua 6:2–3 NLT

X-RAY VISION

So you're the commander in chief now. Picture it: huge army ready to fight, swords and spears sharpened, your men eager to conquer. After all, they've spent their whole lives wandering around outside this land waiting for the word to attack. So you ... order them to line up and walk silently around the city. That's the way you'd do it, right? Something tells me this battle plan wasn't what Joshua originally had in mind. I'll bet the enemy army laughed and tried to spit down on them.

But God made His point—to the Israelites and to us. He wants us to fight our battles differently. Overcoming our enemies and obstacles isn't about our muscle and strength. It's about God. It's about trusting Him to guide and help us. The Bible tells us later that our battles are more spiritual than human; our weapons are prayer and God's Word and our belief in Him. Read about it in Ephesians 6:10–18.

How are you fighting? Are you willing to try it God's way? Turn to Him when you run into a brick wall. He has ways to take down walls that may sound unusual—but they are way more trustworthy.

YOUR MISSION

1. Memorize Joshua 1:9. Say it out loud when you're nervous about a challenge.

2. Build a model of Jericho. March around it while you pray about a problem of your own. Then destroy the city however you want.

3. Try it God's way. Try following one of God's commands that sound weird to you, such as loving your enemies or praying for people who pick on you.

YOUR DEBRIEF

- How do you think the Israelites felt as they were marching silently around Jericho?

- How do you think they felt after the walls crashed down?

- What does God care most about: beating our enemies or teaching us that we can trust Him?

MISSION ACCOMPLISHED

What did you learn?

What do you want to remember?

TO THE RIVER!

THE CANAANITES TRY TO RETREAT. BUT THE KISHON RIVER IS ALREADY OVERFLOWING ITS BANKS. AND THE CANAANITES WHO TRY TO SWIM TO SAFETY SINK UNDER THE WEIGHT OF THEIR HEAVY ARMOR.

SISERA TRIES TO ESCAPE. ON THE WAY HE STOPS TO REST IN A TENT THAT HE THINKS IS FRIENDLY. BUT THE WOMAN WHO LIVES THERE, JAEL, IS LOYAL TO ISRAEL AND KILLS SISERA WHILE HE IS ASLEEP.

WHEN DEBORAH LEARNS THAT THE CANAANITES HAVE BEEN DEFEATED, SHE SINGS A SONG OF VICTORY ...

IN THE HEAVENS, EVEN THE STARS FIGHT FOR THE LORD. MAY ALL THE LORD'S ENEMIES PERISH. AND MAY THOSE WHO LOVE THE LORD BE LIKE THE SUN SHINING IN ALL ITS MIGHT.

THE PEOPLE REJOICE AND SING PRAISES TOO. AND FOR 40 YEARS THERE IS PEACE IN ISRAEL. FAMILIES WORK IN THEIR FIELDS AND HARVEST THEIR CROPS. BUT IN TIME THEY AGAIN FORGET GOD AND FIND THEMSELVES IN MORE TROUBLE THAN EVER BEFORE.

KEY VERSE

"OF COURSE I WILL GO WITH YOU," DEBORAH ANSWERED, "BUT YOU WILL NOT GET CREDIT FOR THE VICTORY. THE Lord WILL LET A WOMAN DEFEAT SISERA." SO DEBORAH WENT WITH BARAK TO KEDESH.

—Judges 4:9 NCV

X-RAY VISION

Girls today can compete on soccer, basketball, hockey, cross-country, debate, and you-name-it teams (at least in our country). They can go to school. They can play in the band. And when they grow up, they can vote, pick a job, and run for president.

You may say, "Duh." But all that hasn't been true for very long. It definitely wasn't true in Bible times. That's what makes Deborah such a special hero.

Women in Bible days were second-class citizens. They didn't have many legal rights and were often treated like property. That wasn't God's plan, but it's the way the culture worked. And none of that stopped God from making Deborah a judge and leader. She was respected so much that all the men came to her when they needed help with raiders and enemies. Even Barak, the one God called to lead the army, needed her help. That was a big deal!

But Deborah had more courage than all the men. God chose an unlikely leader, and she came through when it counted because she trusted what God said. When it comes to accomplishing great things, it's much more about believing in God's strength than popularity, power, or what other people think. God can use anybody—you included.

YOUR MISSION

1. Volunteer. Ask for God's help and be willing to say, "Yes, I'll do it."

2. Guys, read 1 Timothy 5:2. List one way you can show respect to your mom, sisters, and friends who are girls.

3. Girls, read 1 Timothy 5:1. List one way you can show respect to your dad, brothers, and friends who are boys.

YOUR DEBRIEF

- What would it have felt like to be a woman in Bible times?

- Boys, how do you treat girls? Girls, how do you treat boys?

- Where do you find courage when you're facing a big challenge?

MISSION ACCOMPLISHED

What did you learn?

What do you want to remember?

Cowardly Judge
BASED ON JUDGES 6—7

IN THE YEARS OF PLENTY THAT FOLLOW DEBORAH'S VICTORY OVER THE CANAANITES, THE ISRAELITES AGAIN FORGET GOD. ONE BY ONE, THEY JOIN THEIR NEIGHBORS IN WORSHIPPING THE IDOL BAAL. AT LAST ONLY A FEW PEOPLE IN ALL OF ISRAEL REMEMBER THAT IT WAS GOD WHO HAD RESCUED THEM FROM THEIR ENEMIES.

EVERY HARVEST SEASON, JUST WHEN THE ISRAELITES ARE READY TO GATHER THEIR FOOD FOR THE YEAR, ROVING BANDS OF MIDIANITES STEAL THEIR HARVEST. FOR YEARS, THE DESERT TRIBESMEN TERRORIZE THE ISRAELITE VILLAGES AND RAID THEIR FIELDS.

RUN FOR YOUR LIVES!

IF THEY FIND WHERE I HID MY GRAIN, WE'LL STARVE.

BUT WHEN THE RAID IS OVER ...

IT'S GONE! OUR GRAIN IS GONE!

FOR SEVEN LONG YEARS THE ISRAELITES SUFFER AT THE HANDS OF THE DESERT TRIBESMEN. THEY HIDE OUT IN CAVES AND THRESH THEIR GRAIN IN SECRET PLACES ... BUT THE RAIDERS ALWAYS RETURN.

THEN EVEN MORE FRIGHTENING NEWS COMES ...

THE MIDIANITES ARE COMING AGAIN, AND THEY'RE BRINGING GREAT ARMIES FROM THE EAST.

LIKE GRASSHOPPERS, THE ENEMY SWARMS OVER THE ISRAELITE FIELDS, STEALING GRAIN, CATTLE, AND SHEEP.

ONE DAY A YOUNG ISRAELITE IS SECRETLY THRESHING HIS GRAIN WHEN A STRANGER APPEARS BEFORE HIM.

WHO ARE YOU? WHAT DO YOU WANT?

YOU ARE A MIGHTY WARRIOR, GIDEON. GOD HAS CHOSEN YOU TO SAVE HIS PEOPLE.

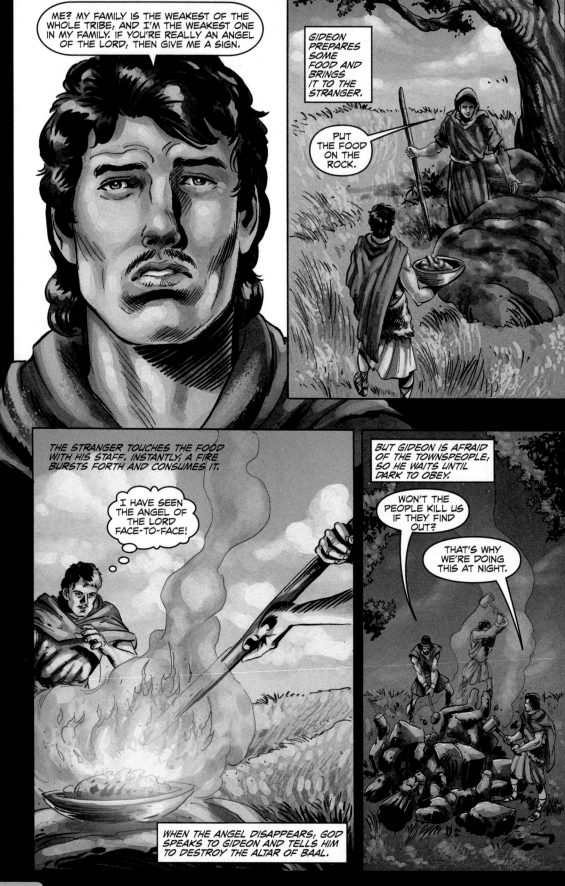

ME? MY FAMILY IS THE WEAKEST OF THE WHOLE TRIBE, AND I'M THE WEAKEST ONE IN MY FAMILY. IF YOU'RE REALLY AN ANGEL OF THE LORD, THEN GIVE ME A SIGN.

GIDEON PREPARES SOME FOOD AND BRINGS IT TO THE STRANGER.

PUT THE FOOD ON THE ROCK.

THE STRANGER TOUCHES THE FOOD WITH HIS STAFF. INSTANTLY, A FIRE BURSTS FORTH AND CONSUMES IT.

I HAVE SEEN THE ANGEL OF THE LORD FACE-TO-FACE!

WHEN THE ANGEL DISAPPEARS, GOD SPEAKS TO GIDEON AND TELLS HIM TO DESTROY THE ALTAR OF BAAL.

BUT GIDEON IS AFRAID OF THE TOWNSPEOPLE, SO HE WAITS UNTIL DARK TO OBEY.

WON'T THE PEOPLE KILL US IF THEY FIND OUT?

THAT'S WHY WE'RE DOING THIS AT NIGHT.

GIDEON CALLS THE LEADERS OF ISRAEL TOGETHER.

WITH GOD'S HELP WE CAN DRIVE THE MIDIANITES FROM OUR LAND. ARE YOU WITH ME?

YES!

YES!

WITH AN ARMY OF 32,000 SOLDIERS, GIDEON MARCHES TO THE HILLS SURROUNDING THE MIDIANITE CAMP.

WHAT A CAMP! THEIR CAMELS OUTNUMBER THE SAND ON THE SHORE.

DON'T WORRY. WITH 32,000 MEN WE HAVE A GOOD CHANCE AGAINST THEM.

BUT GOD GIVES GIDEON MORE INSTRUCTIONS.

GOD HAS SAID THAT IF ANY OF YOU IS AFRAID TO FIGHT, YOU MAY LEAVE NOW AND GO HOME.

MOST OF HIS ARMY DISBANDS. ABOUT 10,000 MEN REMAIN.

BUT GOD WANTS IT TO BE CLEAR THAT VICTORY COMES FROM GOD, NOT THE STRENGTH OF GIDEON'S ARMY. HE MAKES GIDEON WEED OUT HIS ARMY ONCE AGAIN. WHEN THE MEN STOP TO DRINK FROM A BROOK, ANYONE WHO KNEELS DOWN TO DRINK IS SENT HOME.

HOW CAN I WIN A BATTLE WITH SO FEW SOLDIERS?

ONLY 300 MEN ARE LEFT OUT OF GIDEON'S ORIGINAL ARMY OF 32,000. NOW THE ISRAELITES KNOW BEYOND ALL DOUBT THAT ONLY WITH GOD'S HELP CAN THEY DEFEAT THE ENEMY.

HIDE YOUR TORCHES IN THESE PITCHERS. SPREAD OUT ON THREE SIDES OF THE CAMP. WAIT UNTIL NIGHTFALL, THEN LISTEN FOR MY SIGNAL ON THE TRUMPET.

WE'RE READY!

AT GIDEON'S SIGNAL, THE MEN BLOW THEIR TRUMPETS, SMASH THEIR PITCHERS, WAVE THEIR TORCHES, AND GIVE THE BATTLE CRY ...

THE SWORD OF THE LORD AND OF GIDEON!

THE STILLNESS OF THE NIGHT IS SUDDENLY BROKEN BY THE BLARE OF 300 TRUMPETS AND THE CRASH OF BROKEN PITCHERS. STARTLED FROM THEIR SLEEP, THE MIDIANITES RUSH OUT TO FIND THEIR CAMP ABLAZE WITH FLAMING TORCHES.

THOUGH THEY ARE ONLY 300, THE ISRAELITES' TORCHES, HORNS, AND SHOUTING THROW THE MIDIANITES INTO A PANIC. THEY LASH OUT WITH THEIR SWORDS, STRIKING EACH OTHER DOWN. WITHIN MINUTES THEY'VE KILLED MORE OF THEIR OWN MEN THAN GIDEON EVER COULD WITH HIS ORIGINAL ARMY. THE LORD HAS DEMONSTRATED HIS MIGHT ONCE AGAIN.

COWARDLY JUDGE

KEY VERSE

BUT GIDEON ANSWERED, "LORD, HOW CAN I SAVE ISRAEL? MY FAMILY GROUP IS THE WEAKEST IN MANASSEH, AND I AM THE LEAST IMPORTANT MEMBER OF MY FAMILY."

—Judges 6:15 NCV

X-RAY VISION

Ever feel like you're having one of those days, like every day's a bad hair day? Maybe you feel like you just don't measure up, or that you can never get it right. Maybe you feel small, unimportant, or like you really don't matter much.

If so, welcome to Gideon's world. The whole nation of Israel was feeling pretty low. That's because invading Midianites kept roughing them up and stealing all their food. And then there was Gideon. This guy felt like the biggest loser at the bottom of the loser pile. His self-esteem was in the cellar. When an angel told him, "You're the man," Gideon said, "Um, there's got to be a mistake."

Life can beat all of us down sometimes. And our enemy, the Devil, loves to try to make us believe we're nobodies. Check out 1 Peter 5:8. It's a good thing God is way stronger. His message to Gideon is the same for you: *You're strong. You have what it takes. And most important, I'm with you.* God loves to turn so-called nobodies into His heroes.

You matter—no matter how unimportant you feel. God wants to lift you up—no matter how low you feel. You're no mistake. God has plans for you. Ask Him for help to believe it. Then take a step, and see all He does.

YOUR MISSION

1. List the top three superpowers you would choose to have if you could.

2. Lift others up. Spread lots of encouraging words. See how it gives you a boost inside.

3. Give up your doubts. Write down your faults and fears. Then offer them to God by burning them in the fireplace or grill (with your parents' permission).

YOUR DEBRIEF

- How do you view yourself? How does God view you?

- What things are you good at?

- What do you need God's help to do?

MISSION ACCOMPLISHED

What did you learn?

What do you want to remember?

SHARE THE ADVENTURE

Serve someone who has it harder than you. Get your parents to help you visit a nursing home, animal shelter, or soup kitchen. See how much difference you can make.

A Bad Haircut

BASED ON JUDGES 16:1-20

ONE EVENING, SAMSON VISITS THE PHILISTINE CITY OF GAZA..

WHAT IS YOUR BUSINESS IN GAZA?

I HAVE COME TO SEE A FRIEND.

I JUST SAW SAMSON ENTERING A HOUSE DOWN THE STREET. HOW DID HE GET IN?

SAMSON? I DIDN'T RECOGNIZE HIM.

NEVER MIND. CLOSE THE GATE AND WE'LL TRAP HIM IN THE CITY. CALL OUT ALL THE GUARDS! SAMSON WILL NEVER LEAVE GAZA ALIVE.

WHO CAN STOP A MAN STRONG ENOUGH TO CARRY THE CITY GATE? I TELL YOU—

—HIS STRENGTH IS NOT HUMAN!

NEWS OF SAMSON'S ESCAPE FROM GAZA SPREADS THROUGH THE COUNTRY. RULERS OF PHILISTINE CITIES ARE WORRIED AND CALL A MEETING.

SAMSON *MUST* BE CAPTURED. LET'S PUT ALL OUR ARMIES TOGETHER.

I'M NOT RISKING MY ARMY ON SAMSON. WE'VE GOT TO FIND ANOTHER WAY.

I HAVE AN IDEA!

WE KNOW SAMSON HAS MORE THAN MORTAL STRENGTH. IF WE CAN LEARN THE SOURCE OF THAT STRENGTH ...

SAMSON WAKES UP READY TO DEFEND HIMSELF, BUT ...

MY HAIR! IT'S GONE! I HAVE BROKEN MY PROMISE, AND NOW GOD HAS TAKEN AWAY MY STRENGTH.

YOU BROKE THE LEATHER STRAPS, BUT LET'S SEE IF YOU CAN BREAK OUR CHAINS NOW.

SAMSON'S STRENGTH IS GONE! CHAINED AND UNDER HEAVY GUARD, HE IS TAKEN AWAY.

WHAT WILL THEY DO TO HIM?

PUT OUT HIS EYES AND THROW HIM INTO PRISON. OUR TROUBLES WITH SAMSON ARE OVER.

HERE'S YOUR MONEY, DELILAH. YOU'VE EARNED IT.

5,500 PIECES OF SILVER—ALL MINE!

WHILE DELILAH COUNTS HER MONEY, SAMSON IS LED THROUGH THE STREETS OF GAZA—A CAPTIVE IN CHAINS.

HA! THE MIGHTY JUDGE OF ISRAEL IS A WEAKLING NOW!

A BAD HAIRCUT

SO HE TOLD HER EVERYTHING.

—Judges 16:17 NCV

What are your bad habits? Biting your fingernails? Running with scissors? Procrastinating on your homework? Telling lie after lie to try to cover up the first one? Samson had a few of his own that ultimately destroyed him.

You know Samson's story. He's the Bible guy with the most superhero power: insane strength. He's also one of the most tragic characters in the Bible. He had so much going for him. God picked him to rescue His people. An angel even showed up to foretell his birth. But Samson started early on to make bad choices and disobey God's commands. He made a bad habit out of demanding his own way and taking whatever he wanted at the moment. And he especially had a weakness for women who didn't believe in God.

Bad choices have a way of leading to more bad choices. And when you repeat them again and again, you find yourself stuck with a bad habit. No, biting your nails won't ruin you. But habits like losing your temper, talking behind people's backs, or always demanding your own way can lead to bigger and bigger problems.

None of us will ever be perfect, but take a lesson from Samson. Cut off bad choices before they become dangerous habits. Check out your wants—make sure they line up with God's commands in the Bible. Listen to advice from your parents and teachers. Use it to build good habits. Take actions that lead to life, not pain and destruction.

YOUR MISSION

1. Break a bad habit. Have a parent or friend help you get rid of what snags you.

2. Build a good habit. Choose your goal—maybe Bible reading, exercise, or practicing music. Do it for thirty days and you'll have a habit rolling.

3. Avoid your trouble spots. List the ways you get in trouble the most. Then jot down an idea to stay away from them up front.

YOUR DEBRIEF

- What are your bad habits?

- What are your good habits?

- What new habits do you want to form?

MISSION ACCOMPLISHED

What did you learn?

What do you want to remember?

BIG PICTURE PAGE

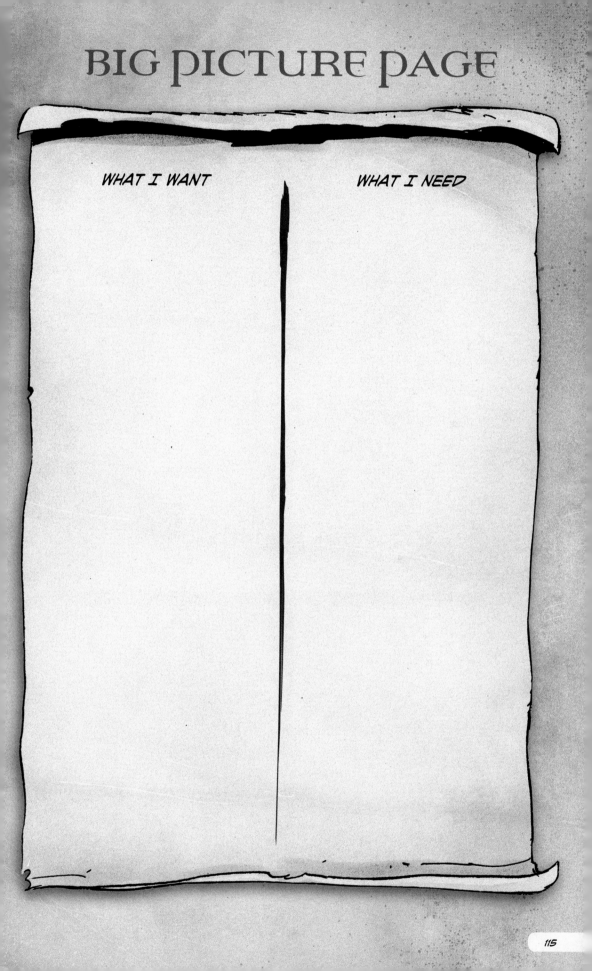

WHAT I WANT

WHAT I NEED

Ruth's Redeemer

BASED ON RUTH

TWO WOMEN LIVE IN A FOREIGN LAND—NAOMI, A JEW, AND HER DAUGHTER-IN-LAW, RUTH, A MOABITE. ALL THE MEN IN THEIR FAMILY HAVE DIED, AND THEY ARE LEFT PENNILESS AND IN NEED.

LEAVE ME, RUTH. I HAVE NOTHING LEFT. I AM OLD. YOUR BEST HOPE IS TO FIND A HUSBAND WHO CAN TAKE CARE OF YOU.

NO, YOU ARE MY MOTHER. WHERE YOU GO, I WILL GO. YOUR PEOPLE WILL BE MY PEOPLE. AND YOUR GOD WILL BE MY GOD. HE WILL TAKE CARE OF US BETTER THAN ANY HUSBAND.

HE DIDN'T TAKE CARE OF MY HUSBAND. MY NAME MEANS "SWEET," AND FOR A WHILE MY LIFE WAS SWEET. BUT NOW THAT GOD HAS ABANDONED ME, THE NAME "BITTER" WOULD BETTER DESCRIBE ME.

COME, WE WILL GO BACK TO ISRAEL, WHERE I HAVE RELATIVES WHO MAY HELP TAKE CARE OF US.

BOAZ QUESTIONS HIS FOREMAN ABOUT PROGRESS ON HIS FIELDS.

... AND ARE YOU TAKING CARE OF THE POOR WOMEN?

YES, AND THERE IS A NEW WIDOW, RUTH FROM MOAB. SHE HAS BEEN LABORING HARD FOR WEEKS TO SUPPORT HER MOTHER-IN-LAW, NAOMI.

NAOMI IS ONE OF MY RELATIVES!

I HAVE HEARD HOW KIND YOU ARE TO YOUR MOTHER-IN-LAW. GLEAN IN MY FIELDS AS MUCH AS YOU LIKE, AND MAY GOD REWARD AND PROTECT YOU.

HE DOES. THANK YOU FOR YOUR KINDNESS.

AT LUNCHTIME, BOAZ IS IMPRESSED WITH RUTH'S FAITH AND WIT.

WHEN THE MEAL IS OVER AND RUTH HAS GONE BACK TO WORK ...

DROP SOME GRAIN ON PURPOSE FOR HER TO PICK UP. MAKE SURE NO HARM COMES TO HER.

DON'T WORRY, BOAZ. SHE WILL BE SAFE, AND SHE'LL FIND ALL THE GRAIN SHE NEEDS.

THAT EVENING ...

LOOK AT ALL THE GRAIN I GOT! NAOMI, YOUR GOD IS GOOD TO US!

WHEN MY HUSBAND AND SONS DIED, I THOUGHT GOD HAD FORGOTTEN ME. NOW I KNOW HOW MUCH HE LOVES ME, BECAUSE HE GAVE ME A DAUGHTER-IN-LAW WHO CARES FOR ME LIKE A DAUGHTER.

I MET THE OWNER OF THE FIELD TODAY. HIS NAME IS BOAZ—AND HE WAS VERY KIND.

BOAZ? HE IS A RELATIVE OF MY HUSBAND'S FAMILY. GOD BLESS HIM FOR BEING KIND TO YOU.

ALL THROUGH THE HARVEST SEASON, RUTH GLEANS IN BOAZ'S FIELD AND TAKES CARE OF NAOMI. ONE EVENING ...

BOAZ HAS SHOWN THAT HE IS KIND TO YOU. AS A KINSMAN, HE HAS THE RIGHT TO MARRY YOU. THE HARVEST CELEBRATION IS TONIGHT. YOU SHOULD WEAR YOUR NICEST DRESS TO THE PARTY, AND THEN YOU SHOULD ASK HIM IF HE—AS YOUR RELATIVE AND REDEEMER—WOULD WANT TO MARRY AND TAKE CARE OF YOU.

BOAZ IS A GODLY MAN, AND I'LL DO WHAT YOU TELL ME.

THE NEWS OF RUTH AND BOAZ'S COMING MARRIAGE SPREADS RAPIDLY THROUGHOUT ALL BETHLEHEM. AT THE WEDDING THERE IS FEASTING, MUSIC, AND LAUGHTER.

ARE YOU HAPPY, MY DEAR?

HAPPIER THAN I EVER DREAMED I COULD BE. GOD HAS BEEN GOOD TO ME.

AFTER THE WEDDING, RUTH AND NAOMI MOVE INTO BOAZ'S BIG HOUSE. LATER, WHEN A SON IS BORN TO RUTH, NAOMI PROUDLY CARES FOR THE CHILD.

I THANK GOD FOR THE DAY YOU LEFT MOAB TO COME WITH ME TO BETHLEHEM. HE HAS TAKEN MY BITTER LIFE AND MADE IT SWEET AGAIN.

I THANK GOD TOO, NAOMI. HE HAS MADE GOOD COME OUT OF OUR SADNESS. HE HONORED US WITH A MAN WHO HONORS HIM. AND NOW I HAVE A BEAUTIFUL BABY.

MY SON IS NAMED OBED, WHICH MEANS "SERVANT." AND MY PRAYER IS THAT OBED WILL SERVE GOD AND HIS PEOPLE.

RUTH'S PRAYER COMES TRUE—FOR HER SON WILL BECOME THE GRANDFATHER OF DAVID, ISRAEL'S GREATEST KING, WHO WILL FREE HIS PEOPLE FROM THEIR ENEMIES.

KEY VERSE

> BUT RUTH REPLIED, "DON'T ASK ME TO LEAVE YOU AND TURN BACK. WHEREVER YOU GO, I WILL GO; WHEREVER YOU LIVE, I WILL LIVE. YOUR PEOPLE WILL BE MY PEOPLE, AND YOUR GOD WILL BE MY GOD."
>
> —Ruth 1:16 NLT

X-RAY VISION

Imagine this: Your friend's whole family gets killed. She drops out of all the after-school activities you share together. Then she moves to a new school where she doesn't know anyone. What would you do? Now you're getting a glimpse of what Ruth and Naomi faced.

Naomi's situation was a little different, but things couldn't get much worse for her. Her husband and sons died, and she lived in a foreign land. In that day, it meant she had nothing—no money, no rights, no land, no way to make a living. Her future was as bleak as a captive mouse at the snake-a-torium. But that didn't keep her daughter-in-law Ruth from sticking with Naomi. Ruth was still young and beautiful. She could have remarried and had a good life. But she was willing to give all that up to help her mother-in-law.

Are you a loyal friend? Do you stick beside a buddy even if you have to sacrifice some fun or popularity of your own? Do you defend her when others start gossiping? Or are you more of a frenemy? Do you turn your back when the friendship is inconvenient?

Sometimes friends start making bad choices. You might need to talk to them about that. If they keep it up and try to drag you down, it might be time to stop hanging out with them as much. Then you can stay loyal by praying for them and letting them know you still care. But every friend makes some mistakes, and being a true friend usually means staying loyal no matter what.

YOUR MISSION

1. Defend a friend next time somebody puts her down to her face or behind her back.

2. Text, message, or call a friend you haven't seen in a long time.

3. Make a list of the traits you want in a friend. Then you act out those traits toward your friends this week.

YOUR DEBRIEF

• Are you as loyal to your friends as you hope they are to you?

• When has someone stuck by your side?

• Who have you let down, and how can you make it up to him or her?

MISSION ACCOMPLISHED

What did you learn?

What do you want to remember?

God's New King

BASED ON 1 SAMUEL 16:1-13

GOD SENDS HIS PROPHET SAMUEL TO BETHLEHEM, WHERE HE IS GREETED BY JESSE, THE GRANDSON OF RUTH AND BOAZ.

SAMUEL! OH NO, WHAT HAVE WE DONE WRONG?

DON'T WORRY, I HAVEN'T COME TO JUDGE YOU. I'VE COME TO GIVE AN OFFERING TO GOD.

JESSE, GOD WANTS ME TO CHOOSE ONE OF YOUR SONS FOR A SPECIAL SERVICE. WILL YOU BRING YOUR SONS TO ME?

OF COURSE.

THIS IS MY OLDEST SON, ELIAB.

HE IS SO TALL AND STRONG! SURELY THIS IS THE ONE GOD HAS CHOSEN.

BUT SAMUEL HEARS GOD'S VOICE: "YOU CAN ONLY SEE HOW TALL AND HANDSOME HE IS. I CAN SEE HIS HEART. HE IS NOT THE ONE."

I'M SORRY. ELIAB IS NOT THE ONE. CALL ANOTHER.

ABINADAB!

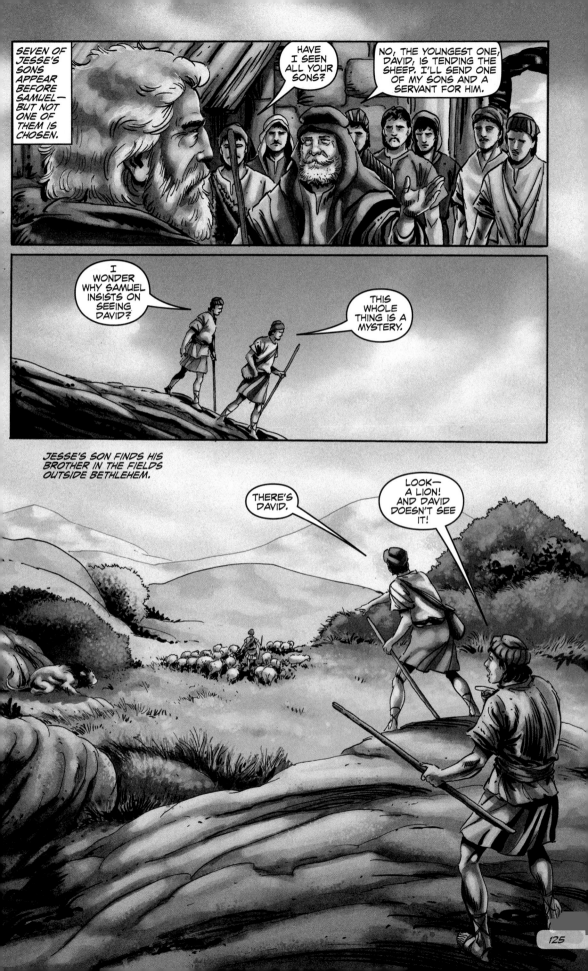

YOU'RE A BRAVE SHEPHERD, DAVID. BUT HURRY HOME, SAMUEL WANTS TO SEE YOU! I'VE BROUGHT A MAN TO STAY WITH THE SHEEP.

THE LORD'S PROPHET WANTS TO SEE ME? BUT WHY?

ON THE HIKE BACK TO THE CITY, DAVID CONTINUES TO WONDER. BUT WHEN SAMUEL SEES THE YOUNG SHEPHERD BOY, HE HEARS GOD SAY, "THIS IS MY CHOSEN ONE."

IN FRONT OF JESSE AND HIS SONS, SAMUEL BLESSES DAVID AND ANOINTS HIS HEAD WITH OIL.

THE LORD BLESS YOU, FOR YOU WILL BE THE NEXT KING OF ISRAEL.

127

KEY VERSE

GOD DOES NOT SEE THE SAME WAY PEOPLE SEE. PEOPLE LOOK AT THE OUTSIDE OF A PERSON, BUT THE Lord LOOKS AT THE HEART.

—1 Samuel 16:7 NCV

X-RAY VISION

If your shirt says this brand, you're cool. If your jeans have that kind of stitching, you're a loser. Got the right accessories? You're in. Get caught with an uncool haircut? You're out.

We do it all the time—judge people with a single glance. We look at the outside of a person and label him or her. It's totally unfair. Unfortunately, it's part of human nature. Even God's prophet Samuel did it. He took one look at the tall, good-looking Eliab and thought, *Now, HE looks like a king!*

But God looks at people differently. He sees us on the inside. He's not impressed by the brand of clothes we wear. He knows that our character counts more than our appearance. He cares what's in our hearts.

God knew that the scrawny young David was His faithful king at heart. And He wants us to look beyond the surface of the people around us just like He does. Peer a little deeper—at the inside of the people all around you.

YOUR MISSION

1. Lose your cool. This week talk to three people labeled uncool or unpopular.

2. Speak up for good. When a friend puts down a person, tell your friend it's not fair to judge. Then point out a positive trait of that person.

3. Lose your labels. Wear a plain shirt or no-name jeans for a day. If someone notices, tell them you're practicing being too cool for brand names.

YOUR DEBRIEF

- How do you feel when someone judges you without getting to know you?

- What person have you misjudged the most?

- Did you feel any different wearing no-name clothes? Why or why not?

MISSION ACCOMPLISHED

What did you learn?

What do you want to remember?

SHARE THE ADVENTURE

Get your friends to help make "Caring Is the New Cool" posters. Or come up with your own positive messages. Ask your principal if you can post them in the hallways.

A Psalming Influence

DAVID DOESN'T KNOW WHEN HE WILL BECOME KING. BUT AS HE GOES BACK TO HIS SHEEP, HE HAS A SPECIAL FEELING OF GOD'S PRESENCE WITH HIM.

THE LORD IS MY SHEPHERD; MY NEEDS ARE SUPPLIED. HE SHOWS ME SAFE PASTURES WHERE WE WALK SIDE BY SIDE.

THAT'S A BEAUTIFUL SONG. BUT I'VE NEVER HEARD IT BEFORE.

I JUST MADE IT UP. IT GETS LONELY OUT HERE, SO I WRITE SONGS AND SING THEM TO THE LORD.

BACK AT THE PALACE, THE MEN GO TO SEE KING SAUL—BUT THEY FIND HIM STARING WILDLY INTO SPACE.

SOMETIMES I THINK THE KING IS GOING MAD. MUSIC SEEMS TO BE THE ONLY THING THAT HELPS.

I KNOW—THE SHEPHERD BOY!

O KING, WE KNOW A YOUNG SHEPHERD WHO PLAYS THE HARP AND SINGS BEAUTIFUL SONGS. IT'S PLAIN THAT GOD IS WITH THE BOY. WOULD YOU LIKE TO HEAR HIM?

SEND FOR HIM.

GOD USES DAVID'S MUSICAL TALENT TO INTRODUCE HIM TO THE ROYAL COURT—THE FIRST STEP TOWARD MAKING HIM KING OF ISRAEL ONE DAY. HERE DAVID CAN LEARN ABOUT KINGSHIP AND GOVERNMENT. HE CAN ALSO WITNESS WHAT LIFE IS LIKE FOR KING SAUL, WHO DOESN'T RELY ON THE LORD.

THE KING IS VERY ILL TODAY, SO HE MAY BE DANGEROUS. DON'T TAKE YOUR EYES OFF OF HIM FOR A SECOND.

QUIETLY, DAVID ENTERS THE KING'S ROOM AND BEGINS TO PLAY. SAUL STARES AT HIM WILDLY, BUT DAVID CONTINUES TO PLAY AND SING OF HIS FAITH IN GOD.

AT LAST KING SAUL RELAXES AND FALLS ASLEEP. AFTER THAT, DAVID IS OFTEN CALLED TO THE PALACE. HIS MUSIC QUIETS SAUL'S TORTURED MIND, AND EVENTUALLY THE KING SEEMS WELL AGAIN—FOR A TIME.

A PSALMING INFLUENCE

KEY VERSE

LET US FIND A GOOD MUSICIAN TO PLAY THE HARP WHENEVER THE TORMENTING SPIRIT TROUBLES YOU. HE WILL PLAY SOOTHING MUSIC, AND YOU WILL SOON BE WELL AGAIN.

—1 Samuel 16:16 NLT

X-RAY VISION

Music is a powerful force. It can pump you up or calm you down. It can rock you like a hurricane or rock you like a baby. Hearing your favorite song can leave you walking on sunshine. Hearing your most hated song can leave you feeling like your face was smeared on sandpaper. A happy song might make you want to hug everyone in sight. An angry song might make you want to stomp on ants.

Even in Bible days music made a big difference. David's songs were the only thing that could calm King Saul. Music was his medicine.

A force like that is something to take seriously, don't you think? The kind of music you choose can affect how you feel, think, and act whether you realize it's happening or not. That's why it's important to pay attention to what you let into your ears—and your heart. Don't let a cool beat distract you from a message that goes against God's Word. Not all your tunes have to be praise songs, but build your playlists out of tracks that honor God and the ways He tells us to live. Doing that will really keep you rocking.

YOUR MISSION

1. Got some talent? Write your own praise song to God. If you're not musical, make it a poem like the psalms.

2. List your favorite songs—and what they're about. Is it stuff that makes God happy?

3. Take a media fast. Go all week without music, TV, movies, video games, or the Internet. See what difference it makes. Choose one, or try for all.

YOUR DEBRIEF

- How do you usually feel after listening to your favorite music?

- Are you paying attention to the musical messages you're letting into your mind?

- Why do you think God gave us a gift as cool as music?

MISSION ACCOMPLISHED

What did you learn?

What do you want to remember?

SHARE THE ADVENTURE

Gather your family to worship God with music. Sing along with your favorite praise songs or play your own.

A Giant Challenge

BASED ON 1 SAMUEL 17

A FEW YEARS LATER, THE PHILISTINES COLLECT THEIR FORCES FOR AN ATTACK AGAINST ISRAEL. SAUL MASSES HIS ARMY AGAINST THEM, AND DAVID'S THREE OLDEST BROTHERS JOIN THE KING'S FORCES.

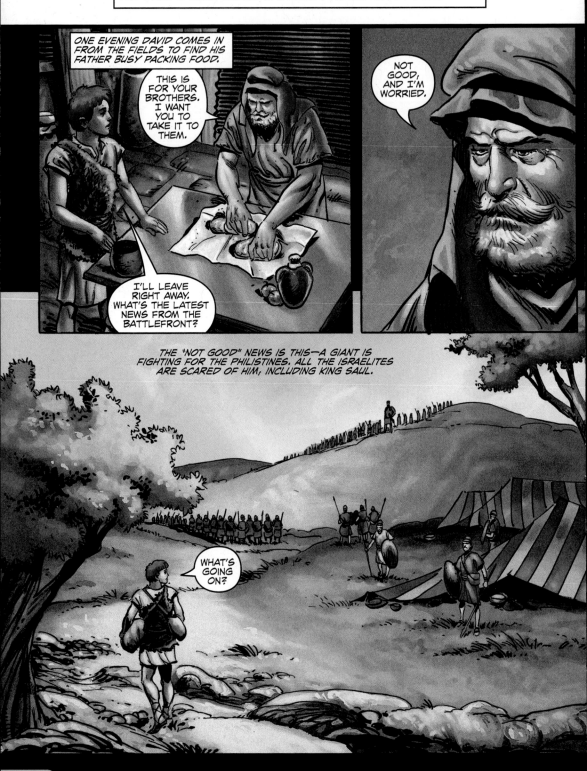

ONE EVENING DAVID COMES IN FROM THE FIELDS TO FIND HIS FATHER BUSY PACKING FOOD.

THIS IS FOR YOUR BROTHERS. I WANT YOU TO TAKE IT TO THEM.

NOT GOOD, AND I'M WORRIED.

I'LL LEAVE RIGHT AWAY. WHAT'S THE LATEST NEWS FROM THE BATTLEFRONT?

THE "NOT GOOD" NEWS IS THIS—A GIANT IS FIGHTING FOR THE PHILISTINES. ALL THE ISRAELITES ARE SCARED OF HIM, INCLUDING KING SAUL.

WHAT'S GOING ON?

ELIAB, DAVID'S OLDEST BROTHER, OVERHEARS DAVID ASKING ABOUT GOLIATH.

WHAT ARE YOU DOING HERE, MOUTHING OFF? WHY AREN'T YOU HOME WHERE YOU BELONG—TAKING CARE OF THE SHEEP?

FATHER SENT ME HERE WITH FOOD FOR YOU. AND I'M NOT THE ONE MOUTHING OFF; THIS PHILISTINE IS INSULTING OUR GOD!

EVER SINCE THE PROPHET SAMUEL CHOSE DAVID INSTEAD OF HIM, ELIAB HAS BEEN FILLED WITH JEALOUSY. NOW HIS SHAME BURSTS INTO THE OPEN.

YOU'RE JUST A SPOILED KID WHO WANTS TO WATCH A BATTLE FOR YOUR OWN FUN.

NO, I JUST HATE TO SEE OUR GOD DISRESPECTED. I'LL FIGHT THE GIANT.

DAVID'S WORDS SPREAD THROUGH THE CAMP.

O KING, THERE IS ONE PERSON WHO WILL FIGHT, BUT ...

BRING HIM HERE AT ONCE!

DAVID ENTERS SAUL'S TENT—BUT SAUL DOES NOT RECOGNIZE THIS YOUNG SHEPHERD AS THE SAME BOY WHO USED TO PLAY FOR HIM.

I AM A SHEPHERD. I HAVE KILLED BEARS AND LIONS TO PROTECT MY SHEEP. THE LORD IS OUR SHEPHERD, SO GOD WILL HELP ME KILL THIS PHILISTINE TO PROTECT OUR PEOPLE.

AN UNTRAINED TEENAGER! YOU CAN'T FIGHT A GIANT! HE'S AN ELITE WARRIOR.

SPOKEN WITH COURAGE AND FAITH. GO, AND THE LORD BE WITH YOU. YOU MAY EVEN WEAR MY OWN ARMOR TO PROTECT YOU FROM THIS MONSTER.

I CAN'T WEAR THIS—I'M NOT USED TO FIGHTING IN ARMOR. BESIDES, MY PLAN IS NOT TO DEFEND MYSELF, BUT TO ATTACK.

I DON'T NEED ARMOR. JUST SOME STONES FOR MY SLING.

A GIANT CHALLENGE

KEY VERSE

BUT DAVID SAID TO HIM, "YOU COME TO ME USING A SWORD AND TWO SPEARS. BUT I COME TO YOU IN THE NAME OF THE LORD ALL-POWERFUL, THE GOD OF THE ARMIES OF ISRAEL! YOU HAVE SPOKEN AGAINST HIM."

—1 Samuel 17:45 NCV

X-RAY VISION

You've probably been the underdog sometime. You might have had to face off against the smartest kid in the class, the girl who always wins the lead role, or the best team. And who hasn't rooted for the player or team nobody expected to make the finals?

David is famous for being the biggest underdog in history. He looked like an underdog on the outside: scrawny kid with a slingshot and a few rocks taking on the superbuff warrior giant who made the entire army's knees knock together. But David didn't see himself as the underdog. He had a different vision from everybody else's. He saw the size of God instead of the size of his challenger.

What are you looking at? God or your challenge? Get yourself ready by practicing like David did guarding his sheep. For you that means learning the Bible and sharpening your skills in school, music, sports, art, friendship, or whatever else is part of your life. When your "giant" pops up, you'll know you're practiced up. You might look like the underdog on the surface, but you'll know God is way bigger. With Him you're the champion!

YOUR MISSION

1. Make your own modern movie version of this story with you in the David role.

2. Build your "giant" out of clay or craft material. Then build a model of you even bigger because of God's power.

3. Carry a "David stone" in your pocket, backpack, or purse. Take it out as a reminder of God's strength whenever you're up against a big challenge.

YOUR DEBRIEF

• What's the biggest "giant" you've ever faced?

• What would you have done in David's shoes?

• What challenges has God helped you overcome?

MISSION ACCOMPLISHED

What did you learn?

What do you want to remember?

The Jealous King
BASED ON 1 SAMUEL 18—19

WHEN THE ARMY RETURNS, SAUL'S GENERAL, ABNER, TAKES DAVID TO SEE THE KING.

YOU SAVED ISRAEL, DAVID. FROM NOW ON, YOU WILL LIVE IN THE PALACE. PRINCE JONATHAN WILL TAKE YOU BACK WITH HIM.

JONATHAN HAS JUST RETURNED FROM THE PALACE. HE IMMEDIATELY RECOGNIZES A KINDRED SPIRIT IN DAVID.

DAVID, I'M PROUD TO BE THE FRIEND OF THE BRAVEST MAN IN ISRAEL. I WANT TO GIVE YOU MY ROBE AND ARMOR AS A SIGN THAT I WILL BE LOYAL TO YOU FOREVER.

THANK YOU, JONATHAN. GOD IS MY WITNESS THAT I WILL BE YOUR FRIEND UNTIL DEATH.

FOR THE REST OF THE MILITARY CAMPAIGN, SAUL GIVES DAVID LOTS OF RESPONSIBILITIES. DAVID EXCELS AT EVERYTHING HE'S ASKED TO DO, AND SAUL PROMOTES HIM TO A HIGH-RANKING OFFICER.

DAVID'S REPUTATION SPREADS, SO BY THE TIME THE ARMY RETURNS HOME, HE IS A HERO.

SAUL HAS SLAIN HIS THOUSANDS—AND DAVID HIS TEN THOUSANDS!

TRIUMPHANTLY, KING SAUL AND HIS VICTORIOUS SOLDIERS PARADE THROUGH THE STREETS. THE WOMEN RUSH OUT OF THE CITIES TO GREET THEM AND SING THEIR PRAISES.

NOT ONLY DOES THE LORD FAVOR DAVID, SO DOES SAUL'S DAUGHTER, MICHAL.

THAT GIVES ME AN IDEA.

DAVID, IT SEEMS MY DAUGHTER IS IN LOVE WITH YOU. AND WHO CAN BLAME HER? YOU ARE THE MOST POPULAR MAN IN THE KINGDOM. BUT SINCE YOU ARE A POOR COMMONER, YOU CANNOT AFFORD THE CUSTOMARY BRIDE PRICE FOR A KING'S DAUGHTER. SO I WILL WAIVE THAT FEE. HOWEVER, TO PROVE YOUR VALOR, YOU MUST KILL 100 PHILISTINES.

THANK YOU, MY KING. I AM HIGHLY HONORED.

YOU MAY BE ABLE TO BEAT ONE GIANT PHILISTINE, BUT 100 OF THEM SHOULD BE ABLE TO KILL YOU.

ONE MONTH LATER ...

WELL? DID YOU KILL 100 PHILISTINES?

NO.

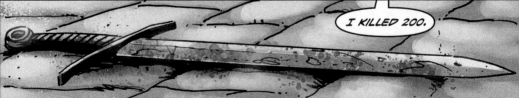

I KILLED 200.

THE JEALOUS KING

KEY VERSE

SO FROM THAT TIME ON SAUL KEPT A JEALOUS EYE ON DAVID.

—1 Samuel 18:9 NLT

X-RAY VISION

William Shakespeare (a sixteenth-century writer you'll know well by high school!) called jealousy the green-eyed monster, and for good reason! Jealousy will eat you up. It's like a flesh-eating virus that will gobble you up from the inside out after the green rises up your eyeballs like in a cartoon.

It's what ate up King Saul. He promoted David into the country's top leadership position. He loved David—until David got more popular than he was. Then Saul's jealousy drove him crazy and wrecked his royal kingship with a spy movie's worth of plotting, deceit, and attempted murder.

Have you let jealousy get the best of you? Don't let the green-eyed monster destroy you and your friendships. Ask God for His love for your friends when they make a better grade or get a cool new outfit. Trust Him when the guy you like likes your best friend—after all, it's not *her* fault he likes her more. Beat back jealousy with thankfulness. Whenever you feel the twinge of envy, thank God for some good gift He's given you—and drive a stake through the heart of the jealousy beast.

YOUR MISSION

1. Let go of jealousy. Decide now to forgive someone you're envying.

2. Try thankfulness. Make a list of good gifts, abilities, and opportunities God has given you.

3. Draw a picture of the jealousy beast. Then draw yourself destroying it with God's help.

YOUR DEBRIEF

- How green are you feeling?

- Who do you envy most? Is it really his or her fault?

- What can you do to show love instead of jealousy?

MISSION ACCOMPLISHED

What did you learn?

What do you want to remember?

Solomon's Wisdom
BASED ON 1 KINGS 3

SOLOMON, THE FIRST OF DAVID'S SONS TO HONOR HIS FATHER AND THE LORD, IS NOW THE HOLY ANOINTED KING OF ISRAEL. HE TAKES THREE IMMEDIATE ACTIONS TO SOLIDIFY THE STATUS OF HIS KINGDOM. THESE THREE STEPS WILL MARK THE REST OF HIS RULE.

FIRST, TO CEMENT AN ALLIANCE WITH EGYPT, SOLOMON TAKES PHARAOH'S DAUGHTER AS A WIFE.

THEN, SINCE HIS FATHER, DAVID, HAD NOT BEEN ALLOWED TO BUILD A TEMPLE FOR GOD, SOLOMON MAKES PLANS FOR A TEMPLE THAT WILL BE A FITTING HOUSE FOR THE CREATOR OF THE UNIVERSE.

FINALLY, HE GOES TO THE ALTAR AT GIBEON TO MAKE SACRIFICES AND SEEK GOD'S BLESSING. THERE HE PRAYS TO GOD AT THE ALTAR ALL NIGHT LONG.

SOLOMON'S WISDOM

KEY VERSE

GIVE ME AN UNDERSTANDING HEART SO THAT I CAN GOVERN YOUR PEOPLE WELL AND KNOW THE DIFFERENCE BETWEEN RIGHT AND WRONG. FOR WHO BY HIMSELF IS ABLE TO GOVERN THIS GREAT PEOPLE OF YOURS?

—1 Kings 3:9 NLT

X-RAY VISION

A genie appears out of your favorite shoe (or out of a lamp if you're a purist for genie stories). You know what happens: you get three wishes, and you can't wish for more wishes. You've thought about this before, so what do you wish for? Money, popularity, fame, clothes, tech gadgets, or games?

That's kind of what happened to King Solomon. But it was no genie. It was the real God. And He told Solomon he could have anything he wanted. Score! But instead of asking for what 99.9 percent of people would ask for—riches, fame, long life—Solomon asked for ... wisdom. He knew that wisdom was more valuable than all that other stuff.

Wisdom is being able to see the big picture. It's more than just being smart. It's knowing how to use your smarts. It's understanding right from wrong and being able to think about the consequences of choices and actions.

It usually takes lots of time and experience to gain wisdom, but it's never too late to start practicing. My old youth leader taught us, "There's right, and there's wrong. But that's not our cue. But rather, what is the wise thing to do?" Sometimes right and wrong are hard to tell apart. Use wisdom to think about consequences and what choices lead toward God's ways. Your wisest choice is to start seeking God and His wisdom now.

YOUR MISSION

1. Learn about wisdom. Read from Proverbs in the Bible every day this week.

2. Ask questions of your parents, grandparents, and teachers. Listen carefully to their answers.

3. Learn from your mistakes. Draw a comic strip about a bad choice you made, but change the story to show how a wise choice would have made a different ending.

YOUR DEBRIEF

- What would you have asked for if you were in Solomon's place?

- Who is the wisest person you know?

- Does wisdom always look smart?

MISSION ACCOMPLISHED

What did you learn?

What do you want to remember?

BIG PICTURE PAGE

COOL SAYINGS AND QUOTATIONS FROM
WISE OR FAMOUS PEOPLE:

(ASK YOUR PARENTS, TEACHERS, OR A LIBRARIAN
IF YOU NEED HELP FINDING SOME.)

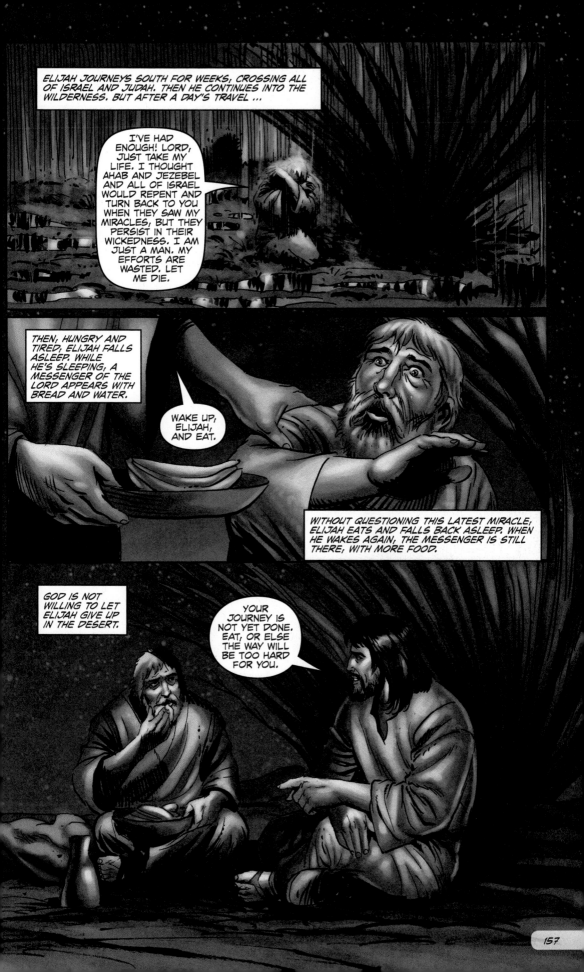

ELIJAH JOURNEYS SOUTH FOR WEEKS, CROSSING ALL OF ISRAEL AND JUDAH. THEN HE CONTINUES INTO THE WILDERNESS. BUT AFTER A DAY'S TRAVEL ...

I'VE HAD ENOUGH! LORD, JUST TAKE MY LIFE. I THOUGHT AHAB AND JEZEBEL AND ALL OF ISRAEL WOULD REPENT AND TURN BACK TO YOU WHEN THEY SAW MY MIRACLES, BUT THEY PERSIST IN THEIR WICKEDNESS. I AM JUST A MAN. MY EFFORTS ARE WASTED. LET ME DIE.

THEN, HUNGRY AND TIRED, ELIJAH FALLS ASLEEP. WHILE HE'S SLEEPING, A MESSENGER OF THE LORD APPEARS WITH BREAD AND WATER.

WAKE UP, ELIJAH, AND EAT.

WITHOUT QUESTIONING THIS LATEST MIRACLE, ELIJAH EATS AND FALLS BACK ASLEEP. WHEN HE WAKES AGAIN, THE MESSENGER IS STILL THERE, WITH MORE FOOD.

GOD IS NOT WILLING TO LET ELIJAH GIVE UP IN THE DESERT.

YOUR JOURNEY IS NOT YET DONE. EAT, OR ELSE THE WAY WILL BE TOO HARD FOR YOU.

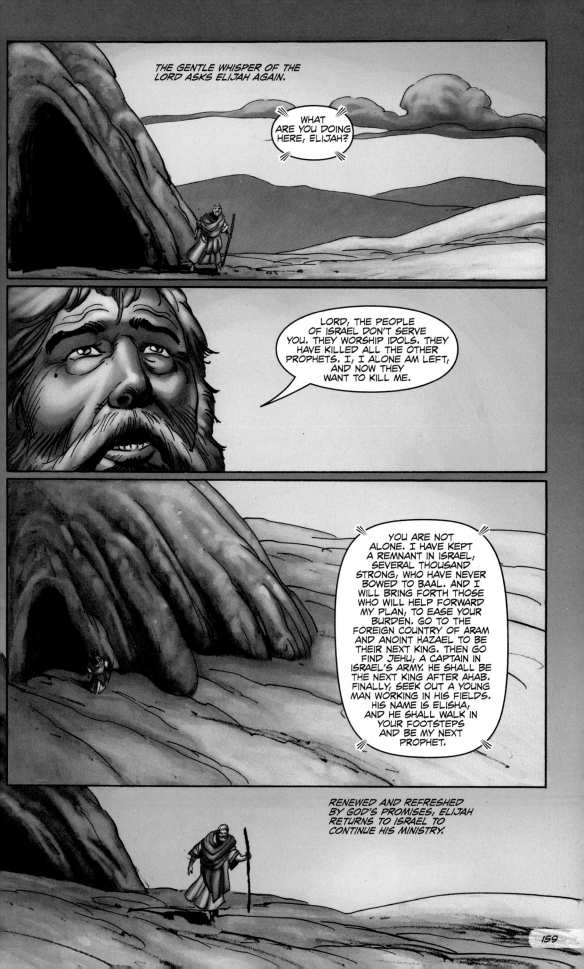

THE SOUND OF SILENCE

KEY VERSE

AND AFTER THE EARTHQUAKE THERE WAS A FIRE, BUT THE LORD WAS NOT IN THE FIRE. AND AFTER THE FIRE THERE WAS THE SOUND OF A GENTLE WHISPER.

—1 Kings 19:12 NLT

X-RAY VISION

Don't you wish you could hear God—out loud? It'd be awesome if you could just pop on your earbuds and tune in your player to your own personal Godcast. Even personal texts or heavenly handwritten messages on a whiteboard would be cool. Guess what? You're not the only one to feel that way.

Elijah is considered one of the most powerful prophets ever. Remember him? Guy who won the battle of the gods on Mount Carmel with fire from the sky. Guy who God kept rescuing because Queen Jezebel wanted to kill him. The dude was part of some serious miracles.

But even Elijah got tired. He wanted to quit. He wanted an answer from God. So God gave him a powerful show: hurricane winds, earthquake, lightning. But God finally spoke in a quiet whisper.

See, God could blow up volcanoes and write messages with clouds, but He doesn't want to have to shout. He wants us to learn to trust Him. He wants us to learn to use our faith—believing with our hearts what we can't always hear with our ears or see with our eyes. He talks to us through His Word, the Bible, and with a quiet voice in our conscience. The more we practice listening, the better we can hear Him.

YOUR MISSION

1. Open your eyes and ears. List ways all around that you see and hear God reminding you that He's here, even if you can't physically see or hear Him.

2. Hear with your heart. What do you love? What makes you feel alive inside? What reminds you of God? Whatever that is—singing, drawing, painting, running—do it while you talk to and listen for God.

3. Trust the source. Have questions or need advice? Look in the Bible for guidance. Use the concordance in the back to look up a topic, or ask your parents where to start.

YOUR DEBRIEF

• What would you do if you did hear God's voice out loud?

• Think of a time you felt God communicating with you. What did it feel like?

• What questions do you want to ask God?

MISSION ACCOMPLISHED

What did you learn?

What do you want to remember?

BIG PICTURE PAGE

SKETCH YOUR FAVORITE SOUNDS.

Dagger in the Night

BASED ON 2 CHRONICLES 24:17-27; 2 KINGS 12

UNDER THE GUIDANCE OF JEHOIADA, THE HIGH PRIEST, JOASH DESTROYS THE TEMPLE OF BAAL AND LEADS HIS PEOPLE BACK TO THE WORSHIP OF GOD. THE HOUSE OF GOD IS REPAIRED, AND FOR YEARS JUDAH PROSPERS. BUT WHEN JEHOIADA DIES, JOASH IS TOO WEAK TO STAND UP UNDER THE PRESSURE OF THOSE WHO WANT TO TURN HIM AWAY FROM GOD. FINALLY, JEHOIADA'S SON, ZECHARIAH, GOES TO THE KING.

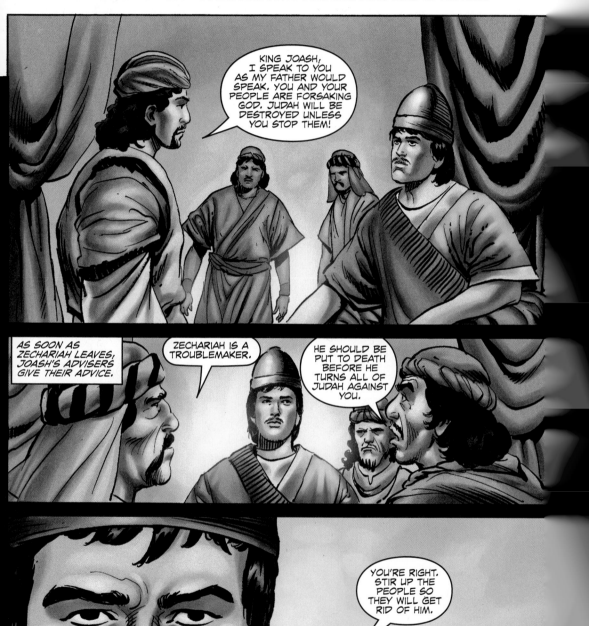

ZECHARIAH'S PREDICTED DISASTER COMES SOON—IN AN ATTACK BY THE KING OF ARAM. DURING THE ATTACK, JOASH IS WOUNDED AND HIS EVIL ADVISERS ARE KILLED. IN AN ATTEMPT TO SAVE JERUSALEM, JOASH TRIES TO BUY OFF THE ENEMY. HIS WOUND IS TOO SERIOUS FOR HIM TO LEAVE THE PALACE, SO HE SENDS A MESSENGER.

GIFTS FROM MY LORD, KING JOASH OF JUDAH. THESE ARE ALL THE RICHES WE HAVE IN OUR TEMPLE. HE ASKS THAT YOU ACCEPT THEM AND LEAVE JERUSALEM IN PEACE.

TELL YOUR KING I ACCEPT HIS OFFER.

HOW IS THE KING TODAY?

NO BETTER, NO WORSE. TOO BAD THE ARAMEANS DIDN'T KILL THE KING ALONG WITH THE MEN WHO ADVISED HIM TO MURDER ZECHARIAH. WITH THEM GONE, WE COULD SAVE JUDAH—IF IT WEREN'T FOR ...

THAT NIGHT, WHEN ALL THE PALACE IS ASLEEP ...

REMEMBER, WE'RE DOING THIS TO SAVE OUR COUNTRY.

SO KING JOASH IS MURDERED BY HIS OWN MEN.

FOR ALMOST 100 YEARS, JUDAH IS RULED BY KINGS WHO WAVER BETWEEN WORSHIPPING GOD AND HEATHEN IDOLS. DURING THIS PERIOD, GOD SENDS PROPHET AFTER PROPHET TO WARN THE PEOPLE OF THEIR WICKED WAYS. SOME PROPHETS DO BETTER THAN OTHERS ...

DAGGER IN THE NIGHT

KEY VERSE

BUT AFTER JEHOIADA'S DEATH, THE LEADERS OF JUDAH CAME AND BOWED BEFORE KING JOASH AND PERSUADED HIM TO LISTEN TO THEIR ADVICE.

—2 Chronicles 24:17 NLT

X-RAY VISION

Advice flies around you like a swarm of bees. Some will give you honey. Others will sting like fire. There's always someone who will tell you what you should do. Friends, teachers, parents, and relatives all give you advice. If you listen closely, you'll realize music, movies, and commercials all give you messages about what to do too. The trick is determining which advice is good and which advice is bad.

King Joash followed the wise advice of the priest Jehoiada for many years, and Jehoiada's guidance always pointed the king toward God's ways. But when the priest died, Joash started to follow bad advice from his advisors. He refused to listen to God's message and had God's prophet killed instead. Everything went downhill from there, and Joash ended up murdered by his own men.

What advice are you listening to? How can you tell if it's good or bad? Bad advice will carry you away from God and His ways. It might encourage you to take selfish or arrogant actions. Good advice agrees with the Bible. It will point you toward God. It will encourage you to live out God's love, peace, patience, forgiveness, and other traits. Pay attention to the advice coming at you. Choose the good stuff.

YOUR MISSION

1. Test some advice someone is giving you by drawing a chart of where it can or will lead.

2. Grade your entertainment. Write down the advice messages from your music, TV, movies, video games, and apps.

3. Make a list of good advisors and bad advisors in your life.

YOUR DEBRIEF

- What's the best advice you've ever followed and what did it lead to?

- What's the worst advice you've followed and what did it lead to?

- Who gives you good, wise advice? Who gives you bad, foolish advice?

MISSION ACCOMPLISHED

What did you learn?

What do you want to remember?

SHARE THE ADVENTURE

Ask your mom or dad to join you in grading your entertainment—and ask them to grade theirs, too. Listen for and talk about the kinds of advice it's giving.

A BURNING COAL

KEY VERSE

THEN I HEARD THE LORD ASKING, "WHOM SHOULD I SEND AS A MESSENGER TO THIS PEOPLE? WHO WILL GO FOR US?" I SAID, "HERE I AM. SEND ME."

—Isaiah 6:8 NLT

X-RAY VISION

What if you get asked to do something risky or new? If you say no, you stay home. You might stay safe, but you miss the adventure. Maybe it's happened to you. You were a little nervous or all-out scared or just didn't feel like getting off the couch. So you skipped the invitation, service project, retreat, mission trip, or team trip—and you missed an exciting adventure.

God opened Isaiah's eyes to an amazing vision of angels. Isaiah saw how incredible God was and how small he was. It was so powerful, Isaiah thought he was going to die. Instead, God asked the young guy, "Who can I send to be My messenger?" It was a question. Get it? Isaiah had a choice. He could say no and stay home scared or bored. Or he could say yes and see God do miracles through him. He could live an intense adventure and become one of Israel's greatest prophets ever. You know what he said.

Every amazing story starts with a yes. Every superhero has a choice. Every princess does too. So do all the everyday heroes around us—will they run or hide from the danger and the bad guys when they feel scared or don't feel like serving? The same is true for God's heroes. And His adventures are the most heroic of all. You have the same choice. What will your answer be?

YOUR MISSION

1. Tell God yes. Then get ready for some adventure.

2. What do you keep saying you can't do? Ask for God's help. Then take a step and try.

3. Draw or paint a picture of what Isaiah's vision must have looked like. Look at it when you're facing a tough decision.

YOUR DEBRIEF

- What would you have done in Isaiah's shoes?

- What adventures have you missed out on?

- What have you been holding back?

MISSION ACCOMPLISHED

What did you learn?

What do you want to remember?

SHARE THE ADVENTURE

Get ready to go. Talk to your parents about doing a service project together or with your church or friends.

Why Do Bad Things Happen to Good People?

BASED ON 2 KINGS 23:29—24:4; HABAKKUK

FOR SEVERAL YEARS, JEREMIAH AND THE KING WORK TOGETHER TO DESTROY IDOL WORSHIP. NEVER BEFORE OR SINCE HAS THERE BEEN A KING LIKE JOSIAH. HE SERVES THE LORD WITH ALL HIS HEART, SOUL, AND STRENGTH. THEN ONE DAY, A MILITARY COMMANDER BRINGS SOME FRIGHTENING NEWS.

THE ASSYRIAN EMPIRE IS FALLING APART, JUST LIKE NAHUM PREDICTED. EGYPT'S ARMY IS MARCHING NORTH. I THINK PHARAOH NECO HOPES TO GRAB WHAT'S LEFT.

IF EGYPT BECOMES THE NEXT SUPERPOWER, THEY WILL WANT TO CONTROL JUDAH AS WELL. I MUST STOP THEM.

STOP EGYPT? BUT IT'S ONE OF THE STRONGEST COUNTRIES IN THE WORLD. AND GOD HAS WARNED ME THAT BABYLON IS THE COUNTRY THAT WILL ONE DAY DESTROY JERUSALEM, NOT EGYPT.

IGNORING JEREMIAH'S ADVICE, KING JOSIAH LEADS HIS SOLDIERS OUT TO DEFEND THE PASS OF MEGIDDO—AND INTO THE PATH OF THE ONCOMING EGYPTIAN ARMY.

IN THE BATTLE, PHARAOH NECO FACES OFF AGAINST KING JOSIAH AND KILLS HIM.

WHEN SOLDIERS BRING JOSIAH'S BODY BACK IN HIS CHARIOT, JEREMIAH IS OVERCOME WITH GRIEF AT THE DEATH OF HIS GODLY KING. HE KNOWS THAT JOSIAH'S DEATH MARKS THE BEGINNING OF THE END FOR JERUSALEM. NOW JEHOIAKIM SITS ON THE THRONE OF JUDAH AS A PUPPET RULER FOR EGYPT. BUT HE DOES EVIL AND LEADS HIS PEOPLE AWAY FROM THE LORD—AND DISREGARDS JEREMIAH'S WARNINGS.

HABAKKUK

AT THIS TIME, THE PROPHET HABAKKUK ASKS GOD SOME TOUGH QUESTIONS. WHY IS THE WORLD SO UNFAIR? WHY WOULD GOD LET A GOOD KING DIE, WHILE WICKED PEOPLE LEAD RICH AND HAPPY LIVES?

WATCH AND WAIT! I PROMISE THAT IN THE END, EVERYONE WILL GET WHAT HE DESERVES. BUT FOR NOW, THE RIGHTEOUS MUST TRUST IN ME AND LIVE BY FAITH.

I WILL TRUST IN THE SOVEREIGN LORD, WHO GIVES ME SURE FOOTING ON TREACHEROUS GROUND.

HOW LONG, O LORD, MUST THE RIGHTEOUS CALL FOR YOUR HELP? WHY DO CRIMES GO UNPUNISHED? ANSWER ME, PLEASE!

IN THE MEANTIME, MORE BAD THINGS HAPPEN TO JUDAH. BABYLON COMES TO POWER JUST LIKE JEREMIAH PREDICTED. THE BABYLONIAN KING, NEBUCHADNEZZAR, CONQUERS EGYPT AND FORCES JUDAH TO SURRENDER. TO ENSURE JEHOIAKIM'S LOYALTY, NEBUCHADNEZZAR TAKES MANY OF THE PRINCES AND JERUSALEM'S FINEST YOUNG MEN AS HOSTAGES.

ALL JERUSALEM SADLY WATCHES ITS FINEST YOUNG MEN BEING MARCHED AWAY. AMONG THE HOSTAGES ARE A YOUNG MAN NAMED DANIEL AND HIS THREE FRIENDS. GOD WILL SOON SHOW HOW HE CAN WORK GOOD OUT OF THIS SAD EVENT.

KEY VERSE

IT IS NOT YET TIME FOR THE MESSAGE TO COME TRUE, BUT THAT TIME IS COMING SOON; THE MESSAGE WILL COME TRUE. IT MAY SEEM LIKE A LONG TIME, BUT BE PATIENT AND WAIT FOR IT, BECAUSE IT WILL SURELY COME; IT WILL NOT BE DELAYED.

—Habakkuk 2:3 NCV

X-RAY VISION

You're trying to do the right thing. You're trying to follow the rules. You're trying to live for God. So why does it seem like the bad kids get away with everything? Why do the mean girls get all the popularity? Why do the arrogant jerks make the team?

That's the kind of stuff the prophet Habakkuk asked God. Israel's good King Josiah followed God but got killed in battle. Then a bad king took over and let the nation get overrun by Egypt. No fair. Why do the evildoers get away with so much while God's followers suffer? The same stuff still happens today. It can be discouraging.

God says stay patient. Don't give up. He'll make it all right eventually. He'll never leave us when the bad stuff happens. He's happy when we keep making good choices to follow Him—especially when life seems unfair.

Maybe we'll see the bad guys get what they deserve; maybe not. For now the world works in broken ways, but God's got a bigger plan. One day He'll fix everything and make it all fair. We might go to heaven before that, where God will right all wrongs. For now, keep doing what's right. God sees it, and someday He'll reward you.

YOUR MISSION

1. Write a poem or song about how God will fix everything someday.

2. Write or draw a comic story about a character who finally gets rewarded for doing the right things.

3. Pray for a mean kid even when he or she gets away with something.

YOUR DEBRIEF

- Why do you think bad things happen?

- If you could fix one big unfairness or injustice around you, what would it be?

- If you were the king or queen of your friends, what would you do to lead them toward God?

MISSION ACCOMPLISHED

What did you learn?

What do you want to remember?

BIG PICTURE PAGE

WHO I CAN HELP

HOW I CAN HELP

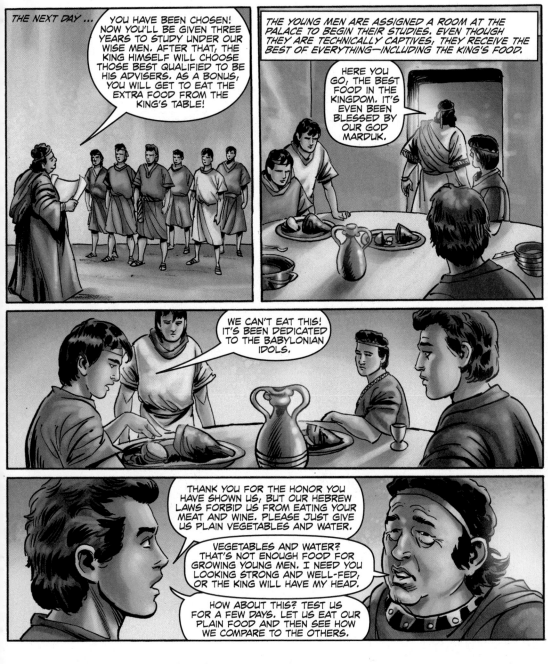

THE NEXT DAY ...

YOU HAVE BEEN CHOSEN! NOW YOU'LL BE GIVEN THREE YEARS TO STUDY UNDER OUR WISE MEN. AFTER THAT, THE KING HIMSELF WILL CHOOSE THOSE BEST QUALIFIED TO BE HIS ADVISERS. AS A BONUS, YOU WILL GET TO EAT THE EXTRA FOOD FROM THE KING'S TABLE!

THE YOUNG MEN ARE ASSIGNED A ROOM AT THE PALACE TO BEGIN THEIR STUDIES. EVEN THOUGH THEY ARE TECHNICALLY CAPTIVES, THEY RECEIVE THE BEST OF EVERYTHING—INCLUDING THE KING'S FOOD.

HERE YOU GO, THE BEST FOOD IN THE KINGDOM. IT'S EVEN BEEN BLESSED BY OUR GOD MARDUK.

WE CAN'T EAT THIS! IT'S BEEN DEDICATED TO THE BABYLONIAN IDOLS.

THANK YOU FOR THE HONOR YOU HAVE SHOWN US, BUT OUR HEBREW LAWS FORBID US FROM EATING YOUR MEAT AND WINE. PLEASE JUST GIVE US PLAIN VEGETABLES AND WATER.

VEGETABLES AND WATER? THAT'S NOT ENOUGH FOOD FOR GROWING YOUNG MEN. I NEED YOU LOOKING STRONG AND WELL-FED, OR THE KING WILL HAVE MY HEAD.

HOW ABOUT THIS? TEST US FOR A FEW DAYS. LET US EAT OUR PLAIN FOOD AND THEN SEE HOW WE COMPARE TO THE OTHERS.

FOR TEN DAYS, THE OTHER TRAINEES EAT THEIR STEAK AND FINE WINE TAKEN FROM THE TEMPLE OF MARDUK. DANIEL AND HIS THREE FRIENDS EAT NOTHING BUT BOILED VEGETABLES AND WATER.

EAT YOUR VEGETABLES

KEY VERSE

DANIEL SAID TO THE GUARD, "PLEASE GIVE US THIS TEST FOR TEN DAYS: DON'T GIVE US ANYTHING BUT VEGETABLES TO EAT AND WATER TO DRINK."

—Daniel 1:12 NCV

X-RAY VISION

Where would you rather eat: at an all-you-can-eat buffet or a prison? Easy choice, right? That's probably what Daniel and his friends were thinking when they got captured and taken to Babylon. But instead of moldy bread and water, they got fancy feasts of steak and wine. *Yes!*

Not so fast. The problem was that the king's food had been dedicated to idols. Daniel, Shadrach, Meshach, and Abednego must have been hungry—they were growing young men. But they wanted to keep themselves pure from anything having to do with fake gods. So they ate only vegetables and drank water—and they became stronger and healthier than all the others.

Nobody's sacrificing your plate in front of little statues, but are you eating at the altar of fast food and junk snacks? Making healthy eating choices is a way to worship God with the body He gave you. Keep yours pure. Eat more fruits and veggies and fewer microwavable snacks. Drink more water and less cola. Choose salad over fries. And don't be surprised when you feel better and grow stronger.

YOUR MISSION

1. Go all week without eating one of your favorite junk foods.

2. Drink water instead of soft drinks all week.

3. Plant something you can eat. Tomatoes, beans, or basil will even grow in a pot.

YOUR DEBRIEF

- How do you feel after going without some unhealthy food?

- Why do you think God cares how you treat your body?

- Do you really think about what you're saying when you pray before eating?

MISSION ACCOMPLISHED

What did you learn?

What do you want to remember?

SHARE THE ADVENTURE

Help your mom or dad cook a healthy meal with fresh ingredients.

THE PEOPLE I ADMIRE MOST:

Facing the Heat

BASED ON DANIEL 3

THANKS TO DANIEL'S MIRACULOUS INTERPRETATION OF THE KING'S DREAM, NEBUCHADNEZZAR PROMOTES HIM AND HIS THREE FRIENDS TO HIGH POSITIONS IN GOVERNMENT. YEARS PASS, AND THE FOUR HEBREW MEN RULE WISELY AND WELL. BUT THE NEWS DOES NOT MAKE THE KING'S OTHER ADVISERS VERY HAPPY.

WHY SHOULD FOREIGNERS GET POWER AND HONOR INSTEAD OF US? WE HAVE TO GET RID OF DANIEL.

NOT NOW—HE'S TOO POWERFUL. BUT IF WE CAN TURN THE KING AGAINST DANIEL'S FRIENDS, WE MIGHT BE ABLE TO CAUSE TROUBLE FOR DANIEL.

THEIR OPPORTUNITY COMES WHEN NEBUCHADNEZZAR CONQUERS JERUSALEM. THE KING DECIDES HE'S GREATER THAN ALL GODS AND BUILDS A STATUE OF HIMSELF. ALL OF HIS OFFICIALS MUST WORSHIP IT— OR BE THROWN INTO A FIERY FURNACE.

THE KING IS PLAYING RIGHT INTO OUR HANDS. HE DOESN'T KNOW THAT THE HEBREWS WILL ONLY WORSHIP THEIR GOD.

DANIEL HOLDS TOO HIGH A POSITION FOR ANY ONE OF US TO REPORT HIM— BUT NOT HIS FRIENDS.

RIGHT! AND TOMORROW WHEN THE TRUMPET SOUNDS FOR ALL PEOPLE TO BOW BEFORE THE STATUE, WE'LL KEEP OUR EYES ON SHADRACH, MESHACH, AND ABEDNEGO.

EAGERLY, THE JEALOUS ADVISERS REPORT TO THE KING.

O KING, THREE OF YOUR HEBREW OFFICIALS HAVE DEFIED YOU. THEY REFUSE TO WORSHIP YOUR STATUE.

WHAT? BRING THEM TO ME AT ONCE!

WORSHIP THE STATUE— OR I'LL THROW YOU INTO THE FIERY FURNACE. TELL ME, WHAT GOD CAN SAVE YOU FROM THAT?

THE GOD WE SERVE CAN SAVE US FROM ANYTHING, INCLUDING FIRE! BUT EVEN IF HE DOESN'T, WE WILL NEVER WORSHIP AN IDOL.

HEAT THE FURNACE SEVEN TIMES HOTTER THAN EVER BEFORE— AND THROW THEM IN!

THE THREE HEBREWS ARE QUICKLY BOUND AND THROWN INTO THE RAGING FIRE.

AAAH! IT'S TOO HOT. I'M BURNING!

FACING THE HEAT

WEEK 28

KEY VERSE

IF WE ARE THROWN INTO THE BLAZING FURNACE, THE GOD WHOM WE SERVE IS ABLE TO SAVE US. HE WILL RESCUE US FROM YOUR POWER, YOUR MAJESTY. BUT EVEN IF HE DOESN'T, WE WANT TO MAKE IT CLEAR TO YOU, YOUR MAJESTY, THAT WE WILL NEVER SERVE YOUR GODS OR WORSHIP THE GOLD STATUE YOU HAVE SET UP.

—Daniel 3:17–18 NLT

X-RAY VISION

It can be hard to stand out in a crowd sometimes, but it can be totally necessary. Have you ever been singled out in class? Maybe you got caught talking. Maybe you had to be the first to share your project. That can be embarrassing, especially if you weren't expecting it. But it can also give you new courage when you discover you can come through in the clutch.

Talk about clutch! Shadrach, Meshach, and Abednego were forced to stand out. When the whole city bowed down to a giant idol, they stood and refused. Talk about some serious peer pressure! The three friends knew what was coming beforehand. They might have been tempted to kneel down—you know, just to blend in and stay alive. But they focused on God—not the towering idol or the mockers or the bad guys who wanted to kill them.

And they stood up when the trumpets blew. They stood in the face of all the people, the bad guys, and the king. Most important, they stood *for* God—and trusted Him to take care of them whether they lived or died.

Chances are, nobody's threatening your life. But are you willing to risk embarrassment to stand on God's side? Concentrate on Him, not anybody or anything else around you. And stand.

1. Go against the flow. Stand for God when everyone is doing something you know is wrong.

2. Draw your own comic strip showing a modern-day version of this story. What's the idol? What would you do?

3. Draw a picture of you in your own fiery furnace—don't forget the angel.

• What's the most tempting "idol" for you?

• What's the hardest situation for you to take a stand in?

• What is your biggest "God saves the day" moment?

What did you learn?

What do you want to remember?

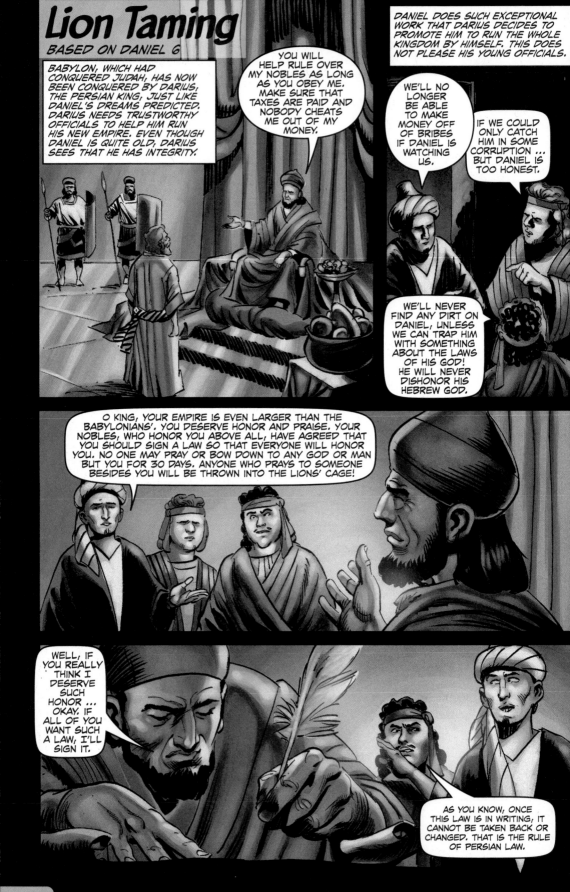

WHEN DARIUS'S NEW LAW IS ANNOUNCED, DANIEL IMMEDIATELY RECOGNIZES THE TRAP SET BY THE DISHONEST ADVISERS.

OH, LORD, HOW THE WICKED TRY TO DISHONOR YOUR NAME AND DISCREDIT YOUR SERVANTS. OH, WELL. I HAVE PRAYED TO YOU, AND NOBODY BUT YOU, FOR MY WHOLE LIFE. I'M NOT ABOUT TO STOP NOW.

DANIEL MAKES HIS WAY HOME ...

... AND GOES TO THE UPSTAIRS ROOM, WHERE THE WINDOWS FACE JERUSALEM. THERE, LIKE HE'S DONE EVERY DAY FOR THE PAST 70 YEARS, HE PRAYS.

SEE—DANIEL PRAYS TO HIS GOD JUST LIKE WE THOUGHT HE WOULD.

GOOD. NOW WE'LL TELL DARIUS.

HAVE YOU NOT SIGNED A LAW FOR A PERSON TO BE THROWN TO THE LIONS IF HE BOWS BEFORE ANYONE BUT YOU?

I HAVE—AND THE LAW OF THE PERSIANS CANNOT BE CHANGED.

DANIEL HAS BROKEN YOUR LAWS. THREE TIMES A DAY HE PRAYS TO HIS GOD—IN FRONT OF A WINDOW WHERE EVERYONE CAN SEE.

DANIEL, MY FRIEND!

I SEE IT NOW. MY ADVISERS TRICKED ME INTO SENDING DANIEL TO HIS DEATH.

THAT NIGHT THE KING CAN'T EAT OR SLEEP. HE PACES BACK AND FORTH THINKING ABOUT DANIEL.

AT DAYBREAK, THE KING RUSHES TO THE LIONS' DEN.

ROLL AWAY THAT STONE!

DANIEL! DID YOUR GOD PROTECT YOU?

O KING, MY GOD SENT AN ANGEL WHO SHUT THE MOUTHS OF THE LIONS! MY GOD FOUND ME FAITHFUL. JUST LIKE I HAVE ALWAYS BEEN FAITHFUL TO YOU, MY KING.

THE KING IS OVERJOYED AND ORDERS A ROPE THROWN DOWN INTO THE DEN. DANIEL IS PULLED OUT.

THEN THE KING SENDS FOR THE NOBLES WHO PLOTTED DANIEL'S DEATH.

YOU SENT DANIEL TO THE LIONS. NOW WE'LL SEE HOW *YOU* LIKE IT! GUARDS, THROW THEM INTO THE DEN!

THE LIONS, WHO HAD SEEMED SO TAME JUST A MOMENT BEFORE, IMMEDIATELY DEVOUR THE WICKED ADVISERS.

KING DARIUS MAKES A DECREE ...

I, DARIUS, COMMAND ALL PEOPLE IN THIS KINGDOM TO HONOR THE GOD THAT DANIEL WORSHIPS AND SERVES.

AND FOR THE REST OF HIS LIFE, DANIEL HELPS THE PERSIANS RULE BABYLON, THE COUNTRY HE ENTERED AS A CAPTIVE. AGAINST ALL ODDS, HE BOLDLY STANDS FOR GOD—AND GOD REWARDS HIM.

LION TAMING

WEEK 29

KEY VERSE

EVEN THOUGH DANIEL KNEW THAT THE NEW LAW HAD BEEN WRITTEN, HE WENT TO PRAY IN AN UPSTAIRS ROOM IN HIS HOUSE, WHICH HAD WINDOWS THAT OPENED TOWARD JERUSALEM. THREE TIMES EACH DAY DANIEL WOULD KNEEL DOWN TO PRAY AND THANK GOD, JUST AS HE ALWAYS HAD DONE.

—Daniel 6:10 NCV

X-RAY VISION

Talking to your friends is fun. You joke and laugh together. You share secrets. You call each other on the phone. You probably text if you have your own phones. You get in trouble at school because you can't keep from talking, even when you're supposed to be working.

Talking is how you get to know your friends. You find out what they like and dislike. You tell each other how you're feeling. You learn new things from each other. You share ups and downs.

Prayer is talking to God. It's how you communicate and get to know God. It's like hanging out with a friend. That's why Daniel wasn't about to stop talking to God—even though it might cost him his life.

Prayer is way more than saying grace before meals or repeating a poem at bedtime. It's not boring—it's way better. It can be an adventure. It's a conversation. It's a hangout session with your best friend, who happens to be the ruler of the universe. It involves you listening, too—not for a voice out loud but for quiet guidance in your conscience. Prayer doesn't always have to be long. It can be a silent thank-you or a sudden "Wow, God, that's so cool!" Sometimes it's even more a feeling in your heart than actual words. It's pretty amazing that God has given us a direct line to Himself! Use it often.

YOUR MISSION

1. Pick a time to talk to God every day this week. Write it on your calendar if you keep one.

2. Make a list of items to talk to God about: questions, requests, thanks. Write down how God answers each.

3. Talk to God while you walk, run, or ride a bike.

YOUR DEBRIEF

- Is it easier for you to sit still and pray or to talk to God while doing something active?

- Is it easier for you to pray out loud or silently?

- What would you do if the law said you couldn't pray?

MISSION ACCOMPLISHED

What did you learn?

What do you want to remember?

BIG PICTURE PAGE

I'M GOING TO KEEP GOING WHEN ...

If I Perish, I Perish

BASED ON ESTHER 4

WHEN MORDECAI HEARS THE ORDERS, HE DRESSES IN SACKCLOTH AND POURS ASHES OVER HIS HEAD TO SHOW HIS GRIEF. THEN HE VISITS ESTHER, WHO HE HOPES WILL BE ABLE TO DO SOMETHING.

WHAT ARE YOU DOING HERE IN SACKCLOTH? DON'T YOU KNOW IT'S AGAINST THE LAW TO SHOW MOURNING IN THE KING'S PALACE? YOU COULD BE KILLED!

I AM TO BE KILLED ANYWAY—ALONG WITH ALL OF OUR PEOPLE.

WHAT? WHY?

THE KING HAS PASSED A NEW LAW ORDERING THAT ALL JEWS ARE TO BE KILLED. IT MUST BE HAMAN'S DOING. HIS PEOPLE HAVE HATED OUR PEOPLE EVER SINCE THE TIME OF KING SAUL.

YOU MUST GO TO THE KING AND ASK HIM TO SPARE THE JEWS.

I SHOULD GO SEE THE KING? THE KING HAS ONE RULE ABOUT ANYONE WHO APPROACHES HIM WITHOUT BEING INVITED: DEATH! UNLESS HE DECIDES TO HOLD OUT HIS SCEPTER. AND THE KING HASN'T CALLED FOR ME IN A MONTH. IF I GO TO KING XERXES UNINVITED, I FACE THE DEATH PENALTY!

IF I PERISH, I PERISH

KEY VERSE

GO AND GET ALL THE JEWISH PEOPLE IN SUSA TOGETHER. FOR MY SAKE, FAST; DO NOT EAT OR DRINK FOR THREE DAYS, NIGHT AND DAY. I AND MY SERVANT GIRLS WILL ALSO FAST. THEN I WILL GO TO THE KING, EVEN THOUGH IT IS AGAINST THE LAW, AND IF I DIE, I DIE.

—Esther 4:16 NCV

X-RAY VISION

What if Christopher Columbus had never set sail? What if Benjamin Franklin and Thomas Jefferson hadn't signed the Declaration of Independence? What if Rosa Parks hadn't refused to give up her seat on the bus? Or the *Apollo 11* astronauts hadn't climbed into their moon lander?

What if Queen Esther hadn't risked her life? Well, the Jewish people in Persia would have all been killed.

Sometimes you've got to take a chance. Sometimes you're the one like Esther—the only one who's in just the right spot at just the right time. Sometimes your action makes all the difference in the world.

That doesn't mean you take stupid risks. Esther prayed and fasted three days for God's guidance before going in front of the king uninvited. And we should ask for God's help and direction too. But when we know the right thing to do, it's time to step up and do it no matter how scared we might feel. That's the time to trust God is with us and go for it!

YOUR MISSION

1. Step up. Use your skill. Take an opportunity. Let God use you.

2. Make a wrong right. Go talk to a parent or teacher to help someone you see being mistreated.

3. Write a story about yourself stepping up to make a big difference. Imagine how God could use you.

YOUR DEBRIEF

- What are you scared of? Why?

- What's the worst that could happen? What's the best?

- Read Esther 4:14. Is there something God has put you in the perfect spot to do?

MISSION ACCOMPLISHED

What did you learn?

What do you want to remember?

When in Rome ...

BASED ON MATTHEW 5:41

HERE, OLD MAN! CARRY THIS FOR ME.

THE MIGHTY ROMAN EMPIRE RULES PALESTINE, THE HOME OF GOD'S PEOPLE, THE JEWS. THE ROMANS HAVE APPOINTED HEROD TO GOVERN PALESTINE FOR THEM. HEROD IS CLEVER, BUT HE IS ALSO CRUEL. THE JEWS HATE HIM AND THE ROMAN OFFICIALS WHO WORK FOR HIM.

THAT CHEST IS TOO HEAVY FOR THAT OLD MAN TO CARRY. HE MIGHT HAVE A HEART ATTACK!

THE ROMANS DON'T CARE.

HOURS LATER, THE OLD MAN REACHES HOME.

GRANDFATHER! WHAT'S THE MATTER?

A ROMAN SOLDIER MADE HIM CARRY A HEAVY CHEST TO HEROD'S PALACE.

WHEN IN ROME ...

KEY VERSE

IF A SOLDIER DEMANDS THAT YOU CARRY HIS GEAR FOR A MILE, CARRY IT TWO MILES.

—Matthew 5:41 NLT

X-RAY VISION

We live with great freedom. But what if an invading army conquered our nation and took over? What if they changed our laws however they wanted? What if their soldiers were everywhere in our towns and neighborhoods telling us what to do?

That was real life for the Jews when Jesus came into the world. The Romans ruled. They had tons of soldiers everywhere. They could tell people to do whatever they wanted, and most of the soldiers were mean. The Jewish people hated the Romans. They wanted God to send the Messiah so he could kick out the Romans and make their country strong and free once again. What they got wasn't exactly what they expected.

Jesus brought a way that was different from what anyone expected. He didn't beat up Romans; He said love your enemies. He didn't say revolt; He said serve even more than anyone asks or tells you. He didn't come to rule the world on the outside—yet; He came to save people on the inside.

Jesus's ways still look different. They can even sound weird. Love my enemies? Help people who hate me? Look for ways to serve other people instead of making myself look bigger and better? Yep, different. Those kinds of things make us stand out—in good ways.

YOUR MISSION

1. Do something kind this week for someone you don't really like.

2. Do something this week to help or serve someone else. Bonus if you do it anonymously.

3. Pray all week for enemies, your personal ones and enemies of our country.

YOUR DEBRIEF

- What teachings of Jesus sound weird to you?

- What would it look like to love your enemies?

- What would you have done if you were alive when Jesus came to earth?

MISSION ACCOMPLISHED

What did you learn?

What do you want to remember?

BACK IN NAZARETH, JOSEPH HAS SECOND THOUGHTS ABOUT HIS ENGAGEMENT TO MARY BECAUSE HE DOESN'T KNOW ABOUT GOD'S PLAN FOR MARY AND HER BABY. SO ONE NIGHT, AN ANGEL COMES TO JOSEPH IN A DREAM.

DON'T BE AFRAID TO TAKE MARY AS YOUR WIFE. THE BABY INSIDE HER IS FROM THE HOLY SPIRIT. NAME HIM JESUS* BECAUSE HE WILL SAVE HIS PEOPLE FROM THEIR SINS.

* JESUS MEANS "GOD SAVES."

Birth of a Savior
BASED ON MATTHEW 1:18–2:11; LUKE 2:1-20

JOSEPH BELIEVES THE ANGEL AND MARRIES MARY, EVEN THOUGH HER PREGNANCY SEEMS SHAMEFUL TO OTHERS. ONE DAY THE NEWS COMES THAT THE ROMAN EMPEROR, CAESAR AUGUSTUS, WANTS TO HAVE A CENSUS. EVERYONE MUST GO TO HIS HOMETOWN TO BE COUNTED. EVEN THOUGH MARY'S BABY IS DUE ANY DAY NOW, JOSEPH AND MARY HAVE TO GO FROM NAZARETH TO BETHLEHEM.

WE'VE TRAVELED A LONG WAY. MY WIFE IS VERY TIRED. WE NEED A PLACE TO STAY.

I'M SORRY, BUT BETHLEHEM IS CROWDED BECAUSE OF THE CENSUS. WE DON'T HAVE ANY MORE EMPTY ROOMS.

EXHAUSTED, MARY AND JOSEPH HAVE NO CHOICE BUT TO STAY IN A STABLE. THERE, SURROUNDED BY ANIMALS, MARY GIVES BIRTH TO JESUS. SHE KEEPS HER BABY WARM IN A MANGER FILLED WITH HAY.

THAT SAME NIGHT, SOME SHEPHERDS ARE WATCHING THEIR SHEEP ON THE HILLS OUTSIDE BETHLEHEM. SUDDENLY, A GREAT LIGHT SPLITS THE NIGHT.

WHAT IS HAPPENING?

GOD SAVE US!

DON'T BE AFRAID. I BRING GOOD NEWS FOR YOU AND THE WHOLE WORLD.

TODAY IN THE CITY OF DAVID, A SAVIOR HAS BEEN BORN TO YOU. YOU WILL FIND THE BABY LYING IN A MANGER.

KEY VERSE

THE SAVIOR—YES, THE MESSIAH, THE LORD—HAS BEEN BORN TODAY IN BETHLEHEM, THE CITY OF DAVID! AND YOU WILL RECOGNIZE HIM BY THIS SIGN: YOU WILL FIND A BABY WRAPPED SNUGLY IN STRIPS OF CLOTH, LYING IN A MANGER.

—Luke 2:11–12 NLT

X-RAY VISION

You know the story. You've probably heard it all your life. You've probably acted it out in a bathrobe, glittery wings, or fuzzy sheep costume. You might have heard it so much that you're just, well … used to it. No big deal. *Yeah, yeah, the Christmas story again. Now where are my presents?*

But have you ever thought of the Christmas story as part of the biggest story ever? Have you looked at it as the arrival of the greatest superhero in the universe? This was the Creator and Savior of the world coming to rescue the planet. It was the most powerful force in the universe unleashing His plan to save humanity. It was … a helpless baby?

God's story has always been different. People wanted a conqueror and killer. God sent a servant and sacrifice. Our world's Christmas is about spending and getting—now! God's is about patiently giving. Our stores' Christmas is about cashing in on the season's bling, then moving on to the next big sale. God's is about growing all year—and life—long.

Take a closer look at God's story even if it's not Christmas. There's always something deeper to discover, whether you're wearing an angel costume or not.

YOUR MISSION

1. Write the story of how you would send the Savior to the world. Go ahead, be creative. Then read Luke 2:1–20 and Matthew 1:18–2:11 and compare God's way.

2. Give someone an unexpected gift this week.

3. Give yourself away. Make a list of ways to serve your family, friends, neighbors, and community and start now. If they look at you funny, tell them you're celebrating Christmas all year round.

YOUR DEBRIEF

• Why do you think God sent the Savior as a baby?

• What would you have done if you heard the shepherds' message?

• How can you focus on Jesus this Christmas?

MISSION ACCOMPLISHED

What did you learn?

What do you want to remember?

A Boy in the Temple

BASED ON MATTHEW 2:19-23; LUKE 2:39-52

WHEN KING HEROD DIES, AN ANGEL VISITS JOSEPH AGAIN IN A DREAM.

GET UP! TAKE THE CHILD AND HIS MOTHER AND GO BACK HOME TO ISRAEL. THE ONES WHO WERE TRYING TO KILL THE CHILD ARE DEAD.

JOSEPH TAKES THE FAMILY BACK TO NAZARETH, WHERE HE SETS UP HIS CARPENTER SHOP. JESUS GROWS UP STRONG AND WISE AND FILLED WITH GOD'S GRACE. EACH SPRING, MARY AND JOSEPH TRAVEL TO JERUSALEM TO ATTEND THE PASSOVER FEAST. THEY THANK GOD FOR DELIVERING HIS PEOPLE FROM SLAVERY IN EGYPT HUNDREDS OF YEARS AGO.

ONE YEAR, WHEN JESUS IS 12, THE FAMILY GOES TO THE FEAST AS USUAL.

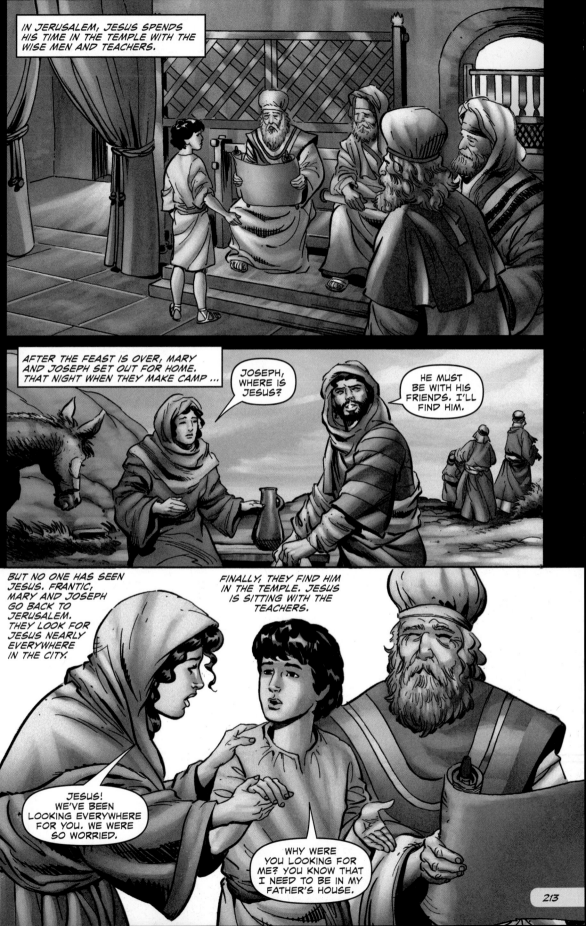

IN JERUSALEM, JESUS SPENDS HIS TIME IN THE TEMPLE WITH THE WISE MEN AND TEACHERS.

AFTER THE FEAST IS OVER, MARY AND JOSEPH SET OUT FOR HOME. THAT NIGHT WHEN THEY MAKE CAMP ...

JOSEPH, WHERE IS JESUS?

HE MUST BE WITH HIS FRIENDS. I'LL FIND HIM.

BUT NO ONE HAS SEEN JESUS. FRANTIC, MARY AND JOSEPH GO BACK TO JERUSALEM. THEY LOOK FOR JESUS NEARLY EVERYWHERE IN THE CITY.

FINALLY, THEY FIND HIM IN THE TEMPLE. JESUS IS SITTING WITH THE TEACHERS.

JESUS! WE'VE BEEN LOOKING EVERYWHERE FOR YOU. WE WERE SO WORRIED.

WHY WERE YOU LOOKING FOR ME? YOU KNOW THAT I NEED TO BE IN MY FATHER'S HOUSE.

YOUR SON HAS BEEN ASKING HARD QUESTIONS. BUT HE HAS GIVEN SOME GREAT ANSWERS, TOO. WE ARE AMAZED AT HIS KNOWLEDGE OF THE SCRIPTURES.

JESUS RETURNS TO NAZARETH WITH MARY AND JOSEPH, WHERE HE CONTINUES TO GROW WISER AND STRONGER. MARY CHERISHES HER MIRACULOUS SON IN EVERYTHING HE DOES. EVERY DAY HE BECOMES MORE PLEASING TO GOD AND TO OTHER PEOPLE.

MILES AWAY IN THE WILDERNESS, ANOTHER YOUNG MAN FOLLOWS GOD'S PLAN. BUT HE DOESN'T HEAR GOD'S CALL IN THE TEMPLE; HE HEARS GOD IN THE DESERT ...

A BOY IN THE TEMPLE

KEY VERSE

"BUT WHY DID YOU NEED TO SEARCH?" HE ASKED. "DIDN'T YOU KNOW THAT I MUST BE IN MY FATHER'S HOUSE?"

—Luke 2:49 NLT

X-RAY VISION

It's your parents' worst nightmare, believe me. Can you imagine how bad they would freak out if they didn't know where you were for three days? They'd call the police, the FBI, the CIA, the Secret Service, and whoever posts those Amber Alerts on TV and highways. They would fear the worst and hope for the best.

And where would you be for three days if you were just hanging out on your own? A friend's house? Your grandparents'? The park or gym? The mall? Jesus was at church. (They called it the temple then.)

It's easy to forget Jesus was a kid too. We're so used to hearing about Him doing miracles and rising from the dead. But this is a great story about when He was around your age. He was studying and learning about God. Yes, He was God, but He was also a human. He still had to learn and grow up just like you.

And He reminds us that it's never too early to make God our priority. It's okay to hang out at those other places we mentioned, but what's most important to you? Your time shows what matters to you. Spend some of yours at church and reading the Bible and serving other people. Just don't hang at church for three days without telling your parents. You don't want to give them a heart attack.

YOUR MISSION

1. Set your priorities. List what's most important to you. Then list how you spend most of your time. Compare the lists.

2. Write a story about you hanging out with Jesus when He was a kid.

3. Pick a book of the Bible to read this week. Ask your parents or youth leader questions about stuff you don't understand.

YOUR DEBRIEF

- What do you think Jesus was like as a kid?

- What do you think His parents thought during and after these events?

- If someone examined your life, how important would they think God is to you?

MISSION ACCOMPLISHED

What did you learn?

What do you want to remember?

JOHN DOESN'T KNOW IT, BUT THE SAVIOR IS IN THE CROWD ONE DAY. JESUS HAS COME DOWN FROM NAZARETH TO HEAR JOHN SPEAK, AND HE ASKS TO BE BAPTIZED.

WHY DO YOU COME TO ME TO BE BAPTIZED?

I'M THE ONE WHO NEEDS TO BE BAPTIZED BY YOU!

JOHN, GOD CHOSE YOU TO INTRODUCE ME TO THE WORLD.

SO JOHN BAPTIZES JESUS. AND WHEN JESUS COMES UP OUT OF THE WATER, THE SPIRIT OF GOD DESCENDS IN THE SHAPE OF A DOVE.

YOU ARE MY BELOVED SON. I AM SO PROUD OF YOU!

GOD HAS SHOWN HIS APPROVAL OF JESUS. THE HOLY SPIRIT'S PRESENCE AT HIS BAPTISM MEANS GOD THE FATHER WILL HELP JESUS WITH HIS HOLY WORK. JESUS GOES INTO THE DESERT ALONE TO THINK ABOUT GOD'S PLAN FOR ESTABLISHING HIS KINGDOM.

FOR WEEKS, JESUS FASTS AND PRAYS. AT THE END OF 40 DAYS IN THE WILDERNESS, JESUS IS VERY HUNGRY.

IT IS THEN THAT HE HEARS THE VOICE OF THE DEVIL SPEAKING TO HIM ...

BAPTIZED

KEY VERSE

AND THE HOLY SPIRIT CAME DOWN ON HIM IN THE FORM OF A DOVE. THEN A VOICE CAME FROM HEAVEN, SAYING, "YOU ARE MY SON, WHOM I LOVE, AND I AM VERY PLEASED WITH YOU."

—Luke 3:22 NCV

X-RAY VISION

Sometimes it happens when you do the right thing even when it's hard. Sometimes it's a simple action that doesn't feel like any big deal. Sometimes it comes from doing your best. Sometimes it's for no reason at all. Sometimes your mom or dad or teacher or coach looks you in the eye and says, "I'm proud of you." Doesn't that feel good?

That's what God did for Jesus—right out loud! It must have been a booming voice. It must have been amazing for John the Baptist and the other people who were there when Jesus got baptized. But it must have been coolest for Jesus. This was God the Father telling His Son, "I love You. I'm so proud of You."

Words like that—words of blessing—will carry you a long way. They give you wings. They give you life.

You have the power to give those kinds of words to others. Look around; the opportunities are everywhere. "Good answer." "Cute outfit." "Great play." "You've got a great smile." "I liked your project." Build people up. Include them. Share kind words freely and often. Give others wings, and you'll probably feel yourself floating too.

YOUR MISSION

1. Give kind words every day this week to someone you don't know.

2. Watch your teammates, bandmates, club mates, project mates, or even teachers. Tell them "way to go" every chance you get.

3. Pay a dollar to a good cause every time this week that you make fun of or cut someone down.

YOUR DEBRIEF

• What are some great words you remember hearing?

• Do you give more compliments or cut-downs?

• When do you think Jesus remembered His Father's words?

MISSION ACCOMPLISHED

What did you learn?

What do you want to remember?

SHARE THE ADVENTURE

Start a compliment club. Stand in the school hallways or walkways and compliment as many people as you can.

Tempted in the Desert

BASED ON LUKE 4:1-13; MATTHEW 4:1-11; JOHN 1:35-51

THE DEVIL DOESN'T WANT JESUS TO DO GOD'S WORK. HE TRIES TO TEMPT JESUS TO MISUSE HIS POWER.

IF YOU REALLY ARE THE SON OF GOD, TURN THESE STONES INTO BREAD.

SCRIPTURE SAYS, "MAN DOESN'T LIVE ONLY ON BREAD, BUT ON THE WORD OF GOD."

THE DEVIL DOESN'T GIVE UP EASILY. SO HE TRIES AGAIN, OFFERING JESUS SOMETHING BIGGER THAN FOOD. THE DEVIL LEADS JESUS TO A HIGH PLACE. IN AN INSTANT HE DISPLAYS ALL THE KINGDOMS OF THE WORLD FOR JESUS TO SEE.

I WILL GIVE YOU ALL THESE KINGDOMS. YOU COULD BE FAMOUS AND POWERFUL. IF YOU WORSHIP ME, IT WILL ALL BE YOURS.

SCRIPTURE SAYS, "WORSHIP THE LORD YOUR GOD. HE IS THE ONLY ONE YOU SHOULD SERVE."

STILL THE DEVIL DOES NOT GIVE UP. NEXT THE DEVIL LEADS JESUS TO JERUSALEM. JESUS STANDS ON THE HIGHEST PART OF THE TEMPLE.

IF YOU ARE THE SON OF GOD, THROW YOURSELF DOWN FROM HERE. SCRIPTURE SAYS, "THE LORD WILL COMMAND HIS ANGELS TO PROTECT YOU."

SCRIPTURE SAYS, "DO NOT PUT THE LORD YOUR GOD TO THE TEST."

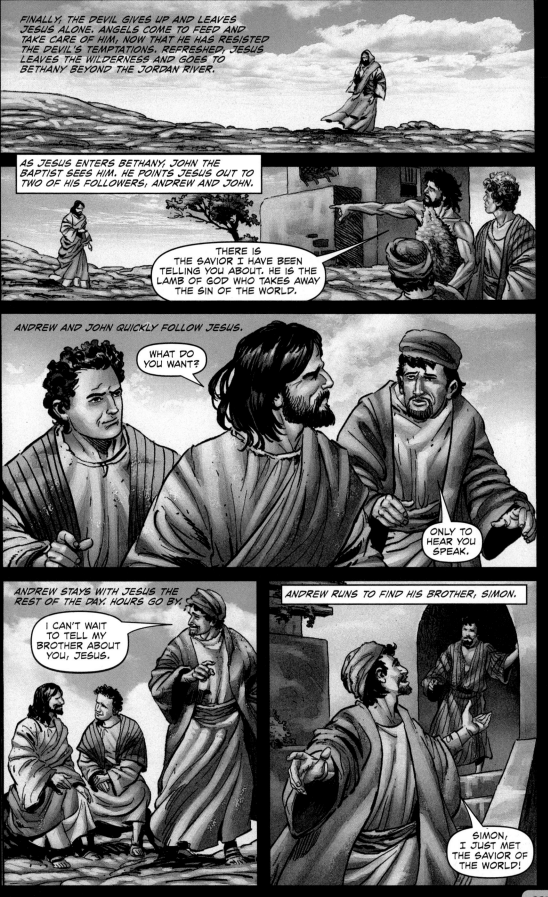

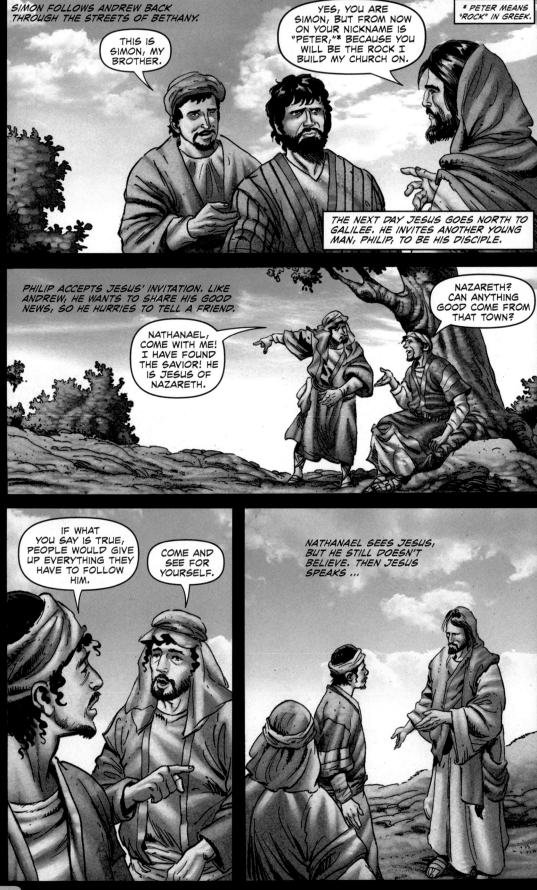

JESUS PROMISES NATHANAEL THAT HE WILL SEE GREATER THINGS THAN SIMPLE FIG TREE VISIONS. HE WILL SEE THE HEAVENS OPEN AND ANGELS COMING DOWN TO EARTH.

KNOWING HE'S FOUND THE SAVIOR, NATHANAEL JOINS JESUS AND HIS FRIENDS AS THEY TRAVEL NORTH TO GALILEE, TO THE CITY OF CANA.

TEMPTED IN THE DESERT

KEY VERSE

> *BUT JESUS TOLD HIM, "NO! THE SCRIPTURES SAY, 'PEOPLE DO NOT LIVE BY BREAD ALONE, BUT BY EVERY WORD THAT COMES FROM THE MOUTH OF GOD.'"*
>
> —Matthew 4:4 NLT

X-RAY VISION

There's a scene in the classic Star Wars movie *The Empire Strikes Back* that almost comes straight out of the Bible. You've probably seen it even though the movie's way older than you. Luke Skywalker has been lightsaber dueling with Darth Vader when Vader drops this verbal bomb on the young Jedi: "I am your father." Darth Vader then tempts Luke to join him on the Dark Side. Together they could rule the galaxy!

Flash back to real life on earth a couple millennia ago. Satan tries a similar move against his archenemy, Jesus. He throws Jesus three temptations, including one to join Satan and rule the world. You know Jesus stands strong in this face-to-face showdown.

Did you know the way Jesus defeats Satan's temptations also gives us an example of how we can beat temptation? Jesus didn't try to argue His way out of temptation. He didn't even try to pray His way out. He used God's Word as His defense. And it worked. We can do the same thing when we're tempted. We can read or quote Bible verses to remind us of God's power and help us walk away. The Bible is way stronger than any lightsaber.

YOUR MISSION

1. Memorize a Bible verse of your choice this week.

2. Say your verse or grab a Bible and start reading the next time you're feeling tempted to do something wrong.

3. Picture your temptation as Darth Vader or some other bad guy—and run from it.

YOUR DEBRIEF

- Do you think it was easy for Jesus to face Satan's temptations?

- How do you usually try to fight temptation?

- Do you know many Bible verses by heart?

MISSION ACCOMPLISHED

What did you learn?

What do you want to remember?

SHARE THE ADVENTURE

Ask your mom, dad, sibling, or friend to check up on you and help you beat an especially tough temptation.

Up on the Roof
BASED ON MARK 2:1-12

JESUS CONTINUES HEALING PEOPLE—EVEN THOSE STRUCK WITH LEPROSY! AS A RESULT, EVERYWHERE JESUS GOES, CROWDS FOLLOW HIM, HOPING TO SEE MORE MIRACLES. ONE DAY IN CAPERNAUM, SO MANY PEOPLE PACK INTO A HOUSE THAT NO ONE ELSE CAN SQUEEZE IN. FOUR MEN BRING THEIR CRIPPLED FRIEND TO SEE JESUS. HE IS PARALYZED AND CAN'T WALK. WHEN THEY CAN'T GET IN THROUGH THE DOOR, THEY GO UP TO THE ROOF.

WHAT ARE YOU DOING?

MAKING A HOLE SO YOU CAN SEE JESUS!

THE FRIENDS' WORK PAYS OFF. THEY LOWER THEIR PARALYZED FRIEND THROUGH THE ROOF RIGHT IN FRONT OF JESUS. JESUS SEES THEIR FAITH AND KNOWS WHAT THE MAN REALLY NEEDS.

YOUR SINS ARE FORGIVEN.

THE PEOPLE ARE AMAZED, BUT SOME OF THE LEADERS, THE PHARISEES, ARE ANGRY AT WHAT JESUS SAYS.

HOW CAN HE SAY SUCH LIES?

ONLY GOD CAN FORGIVE SIN!

JESUS KNOWS WHAT THE PHARISEES ARE THINKING.

WHICH IS HARDER TO DO? FORGIVE A MAN'S SINS OR HEAL A MAN'S LEGS?

TO PROVE I HAVE THE AUTHORITY TO FORGIVE SINS, I WILL ALSO HEAL THIS MAN'S LEGS. STAND UP, PICK UP YOUR MAT, AND GO HOME.

KEY VERSE

THEY COULDN'T BRING HIM TO JESUS BECAUSE OF THE CROWD, SO THEY DUG A HOLE THROUGH THE ROOF ABOVE HIS HEAD. THEN THEY LOWERED THE MAN ON HIS MAT, RIGHT DOWN IN FRONT OF JESUS.

—Mark 2:4 NLT

X-RAY VISION

How far would you go for a friend? How far would your friends go for you? Would they run for cover when the bully grabs you for his next target? Would you stick up for another person when people are posting nasty comments online or talking trash behind her back? Would you give up when keeping a promise to a friend gets hard?

The paralyzed guy in this story had some good friends—"BFF for life" kind of friends. They had his back for real. His backbone didn't work, so they carried him. They knew what—or who—he needed. And they weren't going to let anything, including a crowd or a roof, stop them from getting their disabled friend to Jesus.

We all need each other. Sometimes you're the one who needs the helping hand. Sometimes you're the one who can reach out and give it. Start by being the kind of friend who can be counted on. And you'll find you have friends who have your back when you need it.

YOUR MISSION

1. Pray for a friend each day.

2. Pick someone up. Brag on them online, and compliment them in person.

3. Hang out this week with someone who doesn't have many friends.

YOUR DEBRIEF

- What's the best thing a friend has ever done for you?

- What's the best thing you've ever done for a friend?

- What can you learn from befriending someone with a disability?

MISSION ACCOMPLISHED

What did you learn?

What do you want to remember?

SHARE THE ADVENTURE

Get to know a disabled kid at your school or church. See how you and your friends can help or even just help him or her feel included.

BIG PICTURE PAGE

DIFFERENT IS ...

Sermon on a Mountain

BASED ON LUKE 6:12-16;
MATTHEW 5—8; 13;
MARK 4:1-20

JESUS KNOWS THAT THE PHARISEES ARE PLOTTING TO KILL HIM, BUT HE DOESN'T LET THAT STOP HIM FROM DOING GOD'S WORK. HE GOES UP ON A MOUNTAIN TO PRAY AT NIGHT.

IN THE MORNING, JESUS NAMES 12 MEN TO BE FULL-TIME HELPERS IN GOD'S WORK: SIMON PETER, ANDREW, JAMES, JOHN, PHILIP, NATHANAEL BARTHOLOMEW, MATTHEW, THOMAS, JAMES THE SON OF ALPHAEUS, THADDEUS, SIMON THE ZEALOT, AND JUDAS ISCARIOT.

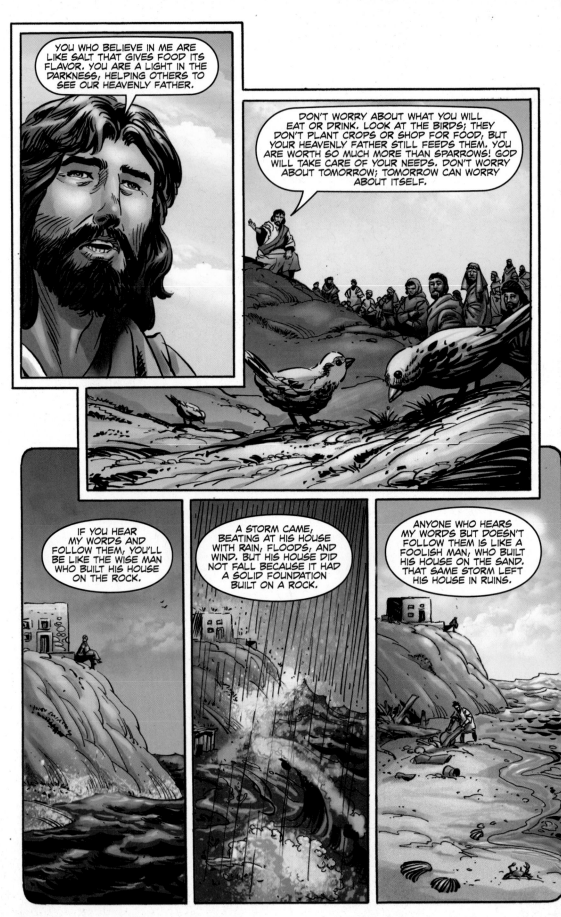

YOU WHO BELIEVE IN ME ARE LIKE SALT THAT GIVES FOOD ITS FLAVOR. YOU ARE A LIGHT IN THE DARKNESS, HELPING OTHERS TO SEE OUR HEAVENLY FATHER.

DON'T WORRY ABOUT WHAT YOU WILL EAT OR DRINK. LOOK AT THE BIRDS; THEY DON'T PLANT CROPS OR SHOP FOR FOOD, BUT YOUR HEAVENLY FATHER STILL FEEDS THEM. YOU ARE WORTH SO MUCH MORE THAN SPARROWS! GOD WILL TAKE CARE OF YOUR NEEDS. DON'T WORRY ABOUT TOMORROW; TOMORROW CAN WORRY ABOUT ITSELF.

IF YOU HEAR MY WORDS AND FOLLOW THEM, YOU'LL BE LIKE THE WISE MAN WHO BUILT HIS HOUSE ON THE ROCK.

A STORM CAME, BEATING AT HIS HOUSE WITH RAIN, FLOODS, AND WIND. BUT HIS HOUSE DID NOT FALL BECAUSE IT HAD A SOLID FOUNDATION BUILT ON A ROCK.

ANYONE WHO HEARS MY WORDS BUT DOESN'T FOLLOW THEM IS LIKE A FOOLISH MAN, WHO BUILT HIS HOUSE ON THE SAND. THAT SAME STORM LEFT HIS HOUSE IN RUINS.

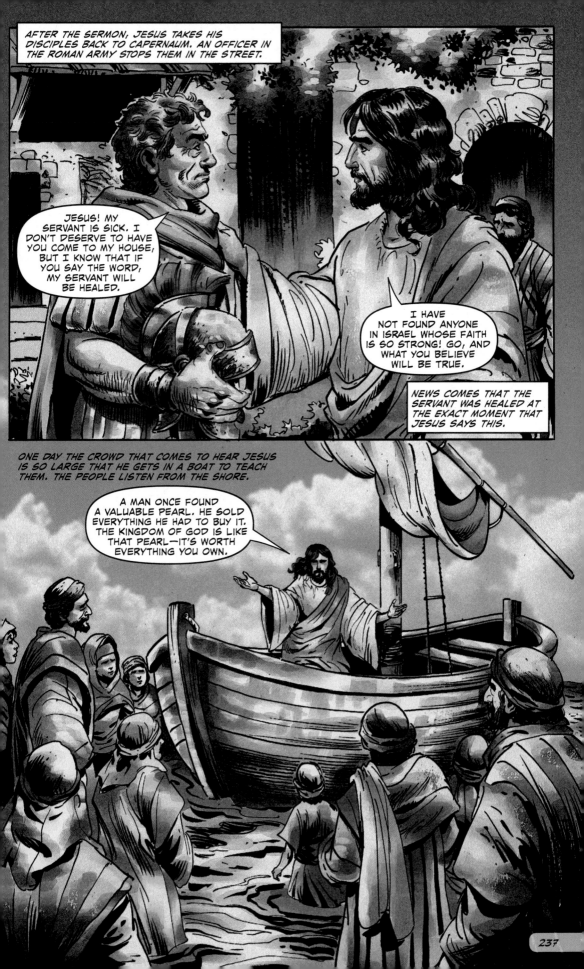

AFTER THE SERMON, JESUS TAKES HIS DISCIPLES BACK TO CAPERNAUM. AN OFFICER IN THE ROMAN ARMY STOPS THEM IN THE STREET.

JESUS! MY SERVANT IS SICK. I DON'T DESERVE TO HAVE YOU COME TO MY HOUSE, BUT I KNOW THAT IF YOU SAY THE WORD, MY SERVANT WILL BE HEALED.

I HAVE NOT FOUND ANYONE IN ISRAEL WHOSE FAITH IS SO STRONG! GO, AND WHAT YOU BELIEVE WILL BE TRUE.

NEWS COMES THAT THE SERVANT WAS HEALED AT THE EXACT MOMENT THAT JESUS SAYS THIS.

ONE DAY THE CROWD THAT COMES TO HEAR JESUS IS SO LARGE THAT HE GETS IN A BOAT TO TEACH THEM. THE PEOPLE LISTEN FROM THE SHORE.

A MAN ONCE FOUND A VALUABLE PEARL. HE SOLD EVERYTHING HE HAD TO BUY IT. THE KINGDOM OF GOD IS LIKE THAT PEARL—IT'S WORTH EVERYTHING YOU OWN.

SERMON ON A MOUNTAIN

KEY VERSE

YOU ARE THE SALT OF THE EARTH. BUT WHAT GOOD IS SALT IF IT HAS LOST ITS FLAVOR? ... YOU ARE THE LIGHT OF THE WORLD—LIKE A CITY ON A HILLTOP THAT CANNOT BE HIDDEN.... IN THE SAME WAY, LET YOUR GOOD DEEDS SHINE OUT FOR ALL TO SEE, SO THAT EVERYONE WILL PRAISE YOUR HEAVENLY FATHER.

—Matthew 5:13–16 NLT

X-RAY VISION

A lighthouse with a ginormous bag over its top is pretty worthless. Runway lights do no good if they're turned off (wouldn't want to be on *that* plane!). Even the moon can't brighten your path when it's covered with clouds. Are you getting the picture?

Salt works the same way. Ever eat saltless potato chips? *Blech.* Or plain popcorn? Way bland. Try some pretzels both ways. It's the salt that's sprinkled on that makes them sing.

Light brightens the way. Salt brings out the flavor and keeps food from spoiling—that's what people used before refrigerators were invented. That's the way Jesus wants His followers to live: shining out, making life tasty, refreshing the world around us.

Don't hide your light—let it blaze. Don't skimp on your salt—shake it out all over. You're filled with God's love. You've been given gifts that can shine on people around you. You're a unique individual who can make your class, family, team, band, community, and world yummy and brighter. So don't be afraid to be different. Shine and shake with all your strength. Let people see God in you, and they'll be attracted to your glow and flavor.

YOUR MISSION

1. Take a taste test. Eat some plain popcorn, chips, or pretzels. Then try the kind with salt.

2. Shine your light. Create some art or a slogan with a positive message, maybe one that goes against something wrong at your school, such as bullying, gossiping, or meanness. Share it with friends and teachers and invite others to join a better way.

3. Pick a "be-attitude" each day from Matthew 5:3–11 and think of one way to practice it.

YOUR DEBRIEF

- How bright and salty are you?

- What skills can you use to brighten and flavor your world?

- What do the traits Jesus blesses in Matthew 5:3–11 mean?

MISSION ACCOMPLISHED

What did you learn?

What do you want to remember?

BIG PICTURE PAGE

GO DOODLING CRAZY!

Walking on Water

BASED ON MATTHEW 14:22-33; JOHN 6:15-21; MARK 6:45-52

BUT GOD SENT JESUS TO BE THE SAVIOR OF THE WORLD—NOT THE CONQUEROR OF ARMIES. WHEN JESUS SEES THAT THE CROWD WANTS TO FORCE HIM TO BE A KING, HE QUICKLY CALLS HIS DISCIPLES AWAY FROM THE CROWD.

WE SHOULD LEAVE BEFORE THIS CROWD STARTS A RIOT. LAUNCH THE BOAT AND CROSS TO THE OTHER SIDE OF THE SEA. I WILL JOIN YOU LATER.

AS THE DISCIPLES ROW ACROSS THE SEA, JESUS GOES UP ON A MOUNTAIN TO PRAY. THAT NIGHT, ON THE SEA OF GALILEE ...

HOW WILL JESUS CATCH UP TO US WITHOUT A BOAT?

GUYS, LOOK! WHAT'S THAT?

KEY VERSE

BUT JESUS SPOKE TO THEM AT ONCE. "DON'T BE AFRAID," HE SAID. "TAKE COURAGE. I AM HERE!"

—Matthew 14:27 NLT

X-RAY VISION

You wouldn't climb out of an airplane. You wouldn't slip out the side of the car while it's doing seventy down the highway. You wouldn't step off a moving train. Would you?

That's kind of what Peter did. The boat was transportation. It's what moved the disciples across the sea. Throw in a storm and the boat was their only safety—at least they hoped it would keep them safe. It could get a little shaky in big storms. And then when they looked and saw—what was it? A ghost? A spirit? A zombie? It couldn't be a human walking on top of the water! That boat felt as safe as a cardboard fort. These tough fishermen suddenly thought they were gonna die.

Right about then is when Jesus told Peter, "Sure, hop on out." And suddenly Peter was walking ... on top of the water! Amazing! As long as he kept looking at Jesus, he was good. But when he started looking around and worrying about what might happen, he started to sink like a fishing weight.

Jesus calls to all of us to keep our focus on Him—to trust Him. What's He calling you to do? Where is He leading you? Don't focus on your problems and worry about what *might* happen. Look at Him and find out what amazing things *can* happen. Talk about cool adventure! Get outta the boat!

YOUR MISSION

1. What have you been afraid to try? Go for it!

2. Write Matthew 14:27 on a card or sticky note. Put it up on your mirror or in your locker as a reminder.

3. Draw your own picture of Jesus reaching out, saying, "Come on." Look at it when you get scared or worried this week.

YOUR DEBRIEF

• Where are you in this story: on the water or in the boat?

• Where is Jesus in this story? Which direction is He heading?

• Why do you think Jesus walked out to the boat?

MISSION ACCOMPLISHED

What did you learn?

What do you want to remember?

249

KEY VERSE

THEN PETER CAME TO HIM AND ASKED, "LORD, HOW OFTEN SHOULD I FORGIVE SOMEONE WHO SINS AGAINST ME? SEVEN TIMES?" "NO, NOT SEVEN TIMES," JESUS REPLIED, "BUT SEVENTY TIMES SEVEN!"

—Matthew 18:21–22 NLT

X-RAY VISION

Have you gotten over it yet? You can't believe what that girl *said*! What that guy *did* makes you mad just thinking about it! In fact, it feels good to feel angry at them. You feel that burning down inside.

But that burning will turn into a blaze, then an inferno, that will swallow you up. Yes, your offender may have been wrong, but you'll be destroyed by holding onto a grudge. If you don't let go, your anger and blame will turn into bitterness. And bitterness will eat you like a cancer.

Peter thought forgiving someone seven times was a lot. Jesus told him to try seven times seventy. In other words, don't even try to keep count. Just keep forgiving. Now, if someone keeps intentionally hurting you, get help. Avoid their actions. Get away from them as best you can. Talk to an adult who can set some limits.

But when you get wronged, it comes down to your choice—sometimes making that choice every time you remember. Forgiveness isn't always easy, but it's freeing. And you've got God's help to lean on. Ask Him for it. Don't hold a grudge and get gobbled. Forgive and live.

YOUR MISSION

1. Apologize today to someone you have wronged.

2. Draw a flip comic strip about revenge on a pad of paper. Erase the end, and finish the story with forgiveness.

3. Build a forgiveness box. Keep it bottomless and put it over your trash can. Write down how you're wronged. Throw it in the box, forgive, and let it go.

YOUR DEBRIEF

- Who is the person hardest for you to forgive?

- Do you forgive people like you want to be forgiven? Or do you hold onto your anger?

- How much has God forgiven you?

MISSION ACCOMPLISHED

What did you learn?

What do you want to remember?

I AM ...

YOU'RE RIGHT. DO THAT AND YOU WILL HAVE ETERNAL LIFE.

THAT'S EASY FOR YOU TO SAY. BUT WHO IS MY NEIGHBOR?

JESUS ANSWERS WITH A STORY ...

A MAN IS TRAVELING FROM JERUSALEM TO JERICHO. ON THE WAY, ROBBERS ATTACK HIM. THEY BEAT HIM UP AND LEAVE HIM FOR DEAD.

A PRIEST COMES DOWN THE ROAD. HE SEES THE WOUNDED MAN AND FEARS THAT THE ROBBERS MIGHT STILL BE NEARBY ...

... SO HE QUICKLY CONTINUES ON HIS WAY.

A LITTLE LATER A LEVITE, AN ASSISTANT TO THE PRIESTS, COMES ALONG. BUT HE HAS IMPORTANT THINGS TO DO IN JERICHO ...

... SO HE, TOO, HURRIES BY.

Who's your favorite team? What team do you hate the most? Some rivalries are legendary: Yankees versus Red Sox, Auburn versus Alabama, North Carolina versus Duke. The hatred is mutual. Sometimes it can be fun, but sometimes it gets out of control.

It had really gotten out of control between the Jews and Samaritans. They couldn't stand each other. They didn't want anything to do with each other. And that's what made Jesus's story about the Good Samaritan so surprising. The Samaritan was the last person anybody would have expected to be the hero of the story—or the example Jesus told them to follow.

God calls us to be like the Good Samaritan. He says love our neighbors as much as ourselves, even the people we don't like. He also says our neighbors aren't only next door. They're all over and around the world. Your neighborhood is just the beginning. In our digital age we can hear about and see stuff anywhere, such as earthquakes in Haiti, tsunamis in Japan, revolutions in the Middle East, and famine in Africa. And with some help from our parents and a few mouse clicks, we can find ways to help people who suffer—whether they're a block or an ocean away. We can love our neighbors no matter how far away they are.

1. Look around for who needs help—in your class, neighborhood, city, country, and around the world. Make a list.

2. Meet a need. Join a group or ministry doing something to help. Volunteer your time or money to join them.

3. Do something—anything. Small actions bring big results. Start today where you are. Talk to your parents about helping globally.

YOUR DEBRIEF

- Who do you pass every day who needs help or encouragement?

- Who are our "Samaritans"—those people we think are different from us?

- What neighbors—near and far—can you help?

MISSION ACCOMPLISHED

What did you learn?

What do you want to remember?

SHARE THE ADVENTURE

Gather some friends and parents and have a fix-it day for old people in your neighborhood or single moms in your church.

IF JESUS AND I HUNG OUT TODAY, WE WOULD ...

A Loving Father

BASED ON LUKE 15:11-32

JESUS LEAVES JERUSALEM AND CONTINUES TO PREACH. THE PHARISEES COMPLAIN BECAUSE HE SPENDS TIME WITH SINNERS. SO JESUS TELLS THEM A STORY ABOUT A MAN WITH TWO SONS. ONE DAY THE YOUNGER SON COMES TO THE FATHER ...

FATHER, I WANT TO RUN MY OWN LIFE. GIVE ME MY SHARE OF YOUR MONEY NOW. I DON'T WANT TO WAIT FOR YOU TO DIE.

IF YOU WANT THE MONEY, YOU MAY HAVE IT. I'LL DIVIDE MY PROPERTY BETWEEN YOU AND YOUR BROTHER.

THE YOUNGER SON MOVES FAR AWAY TO ANOTHER COUNTRY ...

EASY LIVING, HERE I COME!

BARTENDER, I'D LIKE TO BUY A DRINK ...

... FOR EVERYONE!

I'LL BET 300 DENARII.

YOU'RE SO DARING!

AND HANDSOME!

NOW THIS IS THE GOOD LIFE!

IT'S A HUGE HOUSE! TIME FOR ME TO BECOME A HOMEOWNER. ALL MY FRIENDS CAN STAY FOR FREE!

ARE WE HIS FRIENDS?

AS LONG AS HE HAS MONEY, WE ARE!

BUT EVENTUALLY, THE MONEY RUNS OUT. HIS CREDITORS TAKE HIS HOUSE. THE BOY TURNS TO HIS FRIENDS FOR HELP, BUT THEY DON'T WANT TO BE SEEN WITH A PENNILESS LOSER. AT LAST HE IS FORCED TO WORK TAKING CARE OF PIGS TO STAY ALIVE.

MY FATHER'S SERVANTS LIVE BETTER THAN THIS! I'M GOING HOME TO ASK MY FATHER TO LET ME WORK FOR HIM— NOT AS HIS SON, BUT AS HIS SERVANT.

BUT WHEN THE SON REACHES HOME, HIS FATHER RUSHES OUT TO MEET HIM.

FATHER! I HAVE SINNED AGAINST HEAVEN AND AGAINST YOU. I'M NOT WORTHY TO BE YOUR SON.

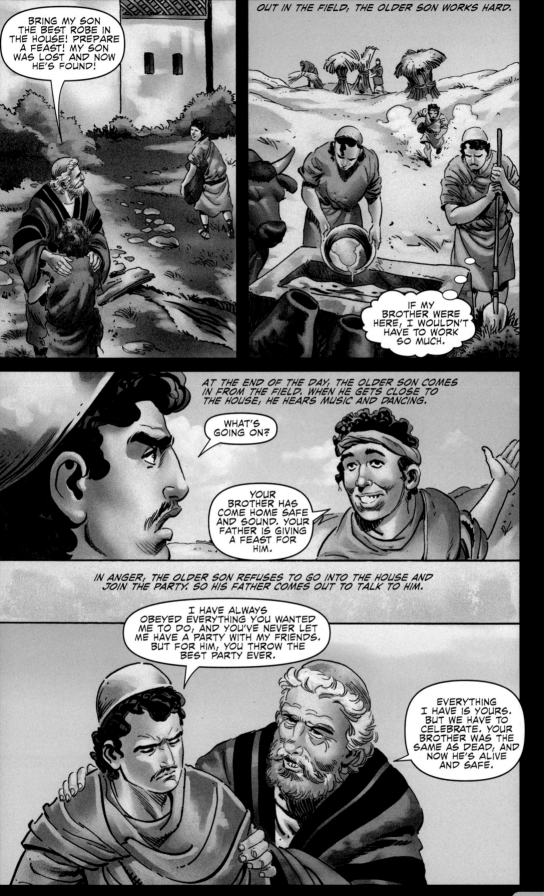

A LOVING FATHER

WEEK 41

X-RAY VISION

Who are you in your family? Are you the responsible one who follows the rules? Or the rebel who's always getting in trouble? Are you the quiet, shy one or the crazy family clown? Are you the big brother or sister, the baby, or somewhere in between?

Jesus told a powerful story about a family with two brothers. You know the one about the prodigal son, the reckless guy who couldn't wait to get his inheritance and then wasted it all away. But there's also the jealous, bitter big brother. And don't forget the father who loves both sons so much that he gives them everything he has and the freedom to choose what to do with it.

There's lots to learn in this story: patience, wisdom, how to choose real friends and handle money, forgiveness, and generosity. But the real question is: Who are you in the story? Are you so impatient to do things your own way that you cause big problems for yourself? Or are you so worried about following the rules that you hate those who don't? Are you jealous when they seem to be having fun and getting away with sin?

God's love is ginormous. There's enough of it for all sorts of people. He wants to help us all learn to follow His good ways and avoid the pain of veering away from them. He gives each of us goodness that we don't deserve—that's called grace. And He wants us to show the same kind of grace to other people. Try starting with your own sisters and brothers.

KEY VERSE

THE YOUNGER SON TOLD HIS FATHER, "I WANT MY SHARE OF YOUR ESTATE NOW BEFORE YOU DIE." SO HIS FATHER AGREED TO DIVIDE HIS WEALTH BETWEEN HIS SONS.... THE OLDER BROTHER WAS ANGRY AND WOULDN'T GO IN. HIS FATHER CAME OUT AND BEGGED HIM.

—Luke 15:12, 28 NLT

YOUR MISSION

1. Invite your brother or sister to do something he or she loves but that you normally don't like to do.

2. Practice patience. Save your money for something you say you want really bad.

3. Get a job. Earn some extra money around the house. Practice saving and spending it wisely.

YOUR DEBRIEF

- Who do you most feel like in the story of the prodigal son?

- What good things has God given you that you did absolutely nothing to earn or deserve?

- Why do you think Jesus told this story?

SHARE THE ADVENTURE

Invite your dad to hang out (or mom if your dad doesn't live nearby).

MISSION ACCOMPLISHED

What did you learn?

What do you want to remember?

Jesus Wept
BASED ON JOHN 11; MARK 10:13-22

WHILE JESUS IS TEACHING IN PEREA, WORD COMES THAT MARY AND MARTHA'S BROTHER, LAZARUS, HAS DIED. JESUS DECIDES HE MUST GO TO BETHANY.

BETHANY? THAT'S TOO CLOSE TO JERUSALEM, WHERE THE PHARISEES WANTED TO STONE YOU TO DEATH. ARE YOU SURE WE SHOULD GO BACK THERE?

OUR FRIEND LAZARUS HAS FALLEN ASLEEP. I'M GOING THERE TO WAKE HIM UP.

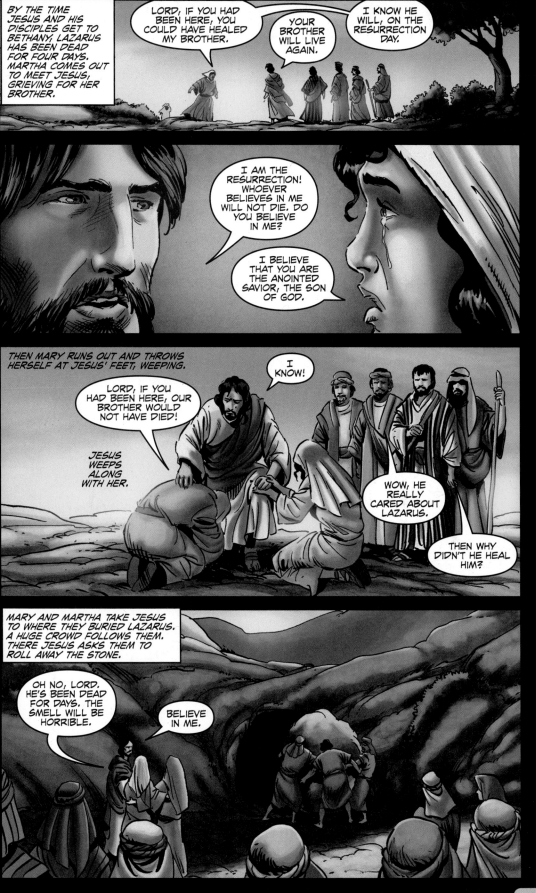

JESUS WEPT

KEY VERSE

JESUS WEPT.

—John 11:35 NIV

X-RAY VISION

Sometimes you can't help but cry. The sadness is just too much, and it can be good to get it out. Sometimes you want to be by yourself. But other times there's nothing better than hugging your mom or a friend while you sob. It helps to know you're not alone.

Jesus knows how you feel. When His good friend Lazarus died, Jesus knew that He would bring him back to life. He knew it would be a great miracle that would help people believe in Him. But when He saw Lazarus's sisters hurting so much, Jesus couldn't help but cry along with them. He felt their sadness. He understood, and it showed.

It might be hard to know what to do when a friend is hurting. It might feel uncomfortable to see them so upset. But often the best thing you can do is to let them know you're there ready to help. That might mean giving a hug. It might be just hanging out with them. It could be a note, voice mail, or text saying you're sorry and available. You don't have to have the answers about why a bad thing happened. Just be ready to listen and stand by their side. You can bring more comfort and encouragement than you realize.

YOUR MISSION

1. Send a note or message today to a friend going through a hard time.

2. Be on the lookout this week, ready to stick by someone who gets his or her feelings hurt.

3. Make something—cookies, a card, a craft—for someone you or your family knows who is facing a sickness, death, tragedy, or other hard time.

YOUR DEBRIEF

- Who do you turn to when you're sad?

- Who needs some encouragement?

- Does it surprise you that Jesus cried? What does that tell you about Him?

MISSION ACCOMPLISHED

What did you learn?

What do you want to remember?

SHARE THE ADVENTURE

Make a banner. Write something like "We love you, _____!" Get all your friends to sign it. Then hang it on the locker of a friend who's going through a hard time.

The Lord's Supper

BASED ON JOHN 13:31—14:31; MATTHEW 26:26-56

AFTER JUDAS, THE TRAITOR, LEAVES, JESUS PICKS UP A PIECE OF BREAD. HE THANKS GOD FOR IT, BREAKS IT, AND GIVES IT TO HIS DISCIPLES. HE SAYS, "THIS IS MY BODY." THEN JESUS OFFERS THEM A CUP.

DRINK FROM THIS CUP, EACH OF YOU. THIS IS MY BLOOD WHICH WILL BE SPILLED FOR YOUR SINS. AFTER I'M GONE, DRINK IT TO REMEMBER ME.

SO JESUS MAKES A NEW COVENANT BETWEEN GOD AND PEOPLE WHO BELIEVE IN JESUS. WHEN WE TAKE THE BREAD AND CUP IN THE NAME OF JESUS, WE REMEMBER THAT GOD SENT HIS SON TO SAVE US FROM OUR SIN AND GIVE US ETERNAL LIFE.

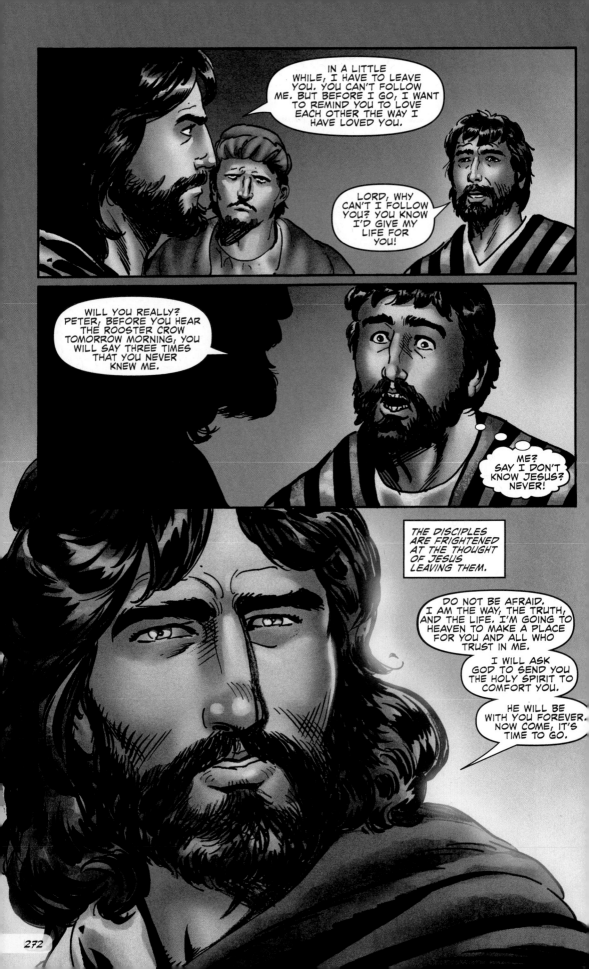

QUIETLY, THEY LEAVE THE UPPER ROOM AND WALK THROUGH THE MOONLIT STREETS OF THE CITY. THEY GO OUT A GATE ON THE EAST SIDE AND WALK ACROSS A VALLEY TO THE GARDEN OF GETHSEMANE ON THE MOUNT OF OLIVES.

JESUS ASKS EIGHT OF THE DISCIPLES TO WAIT WHILE HE TAKES PETER, JAMES, AND JOHN DEEPER INTO THE GARDEN.

THIS IS A SAD NIGHT FOR ME. STAY HERE AND WATCH WHILE I GO ALONE TO PRAY.

OH, DAD, IF IT IS POSSIBLE, PLEASE DON'T MAKE ME SUFFER FOR PEOPLE'S SIN. BUT I WILL DO WHATEVER YOU ASK.

WHEN JESUS RETURNS TO PETER, JAMES, AND JOHN, HE FINDS THEM SLEEPING. HE GOES OFF ALONE TO PRAY TWO MORE TIMES. EACH TIME WHEN HE RETURNS, HE FINDS HIS FRIENDS ASLEEP. THE THIRD TIME ...

WAKE UP! IT'S TIME. THE ONE WHO WILL BETRAY ME IS COMING.

AS JESUS SPEAKS, JUDAS BURSTS INTO THE GARDEN LEADING A CROWD. HE KISSES JESUS TO SIGNAL TO THE SOLDIERS WHO TO ARREST.

GREETINGS, MASTER.

AS THE SOLDIERS GRAB JESUS, PETER SWIFTLY PULLS HIS SWORD AND WILDLY SLASHES OFF THE EAR OF A SERVANT.

PETER! PUT YOUR SWORD AWAY! DO YOU THINK I CAN'T CALL ON GOD TO SEND THOUSANDS OF ANGELS TO PROTECT ME? THE SCRIPTURES SAY THIS HAS TO HAPPEN THIS WAY.

JESUS GENTLY TOUCHES THE SERVANT'S EAR AND HEALS HIM. WHEN THE DISCIPLES SEE THAT JESUS IS LETTING HIMSELF BE ARRESTED, THEY RUN FOR THEIR LIVES. THE SOLDIERS TAKE JESUS BACK TO JERUSALEM—THE SAME CITY HE HAD ENTERED SO TRIUMPHANTLY A FEW DAYS BEFORE.

KEY VERSE

FATHER, IF YOU ARE WILLING, TAKE AWAY THIS CUP OF SUFFERING. BUT DO WHAT YOU WANT, NOT WHAT I WANT.

—Luke 22:42 NCV

X-RAY VISION

You might dread the first day of school, or a test, or maybe having to dress up for a fancy event. If it were up to you, you'd cancel the event, abolish tests from the classroom, and while you're at it, cancel the entire school year altogether. Hmm, if you ruled the world, you might just … outlaw bedtimes, hire a personal junk food chef, imprison all bullies, and never have to clean your room. But guess what? The world doesn't revolve around you. I know, you've heard that one from your parents. It's just the truth. It's not all about you.

Jesus did rule the world. He had the power to do whatever He wanted. He could have changed any rule, destroyed any enemy, made anything appear or disappear, or had a million angels follow His commands with a finger snap. Whatever He wanted.

He didn't want to be beaten, and ridiculed, and cursed, and weighed down by every sin committed by every single villain and average Joe in the history of the world. He didn't want to die. But He knew it wasn't all about Him. It was about you and me, and His Father, and His bigger plan to rescue humanity. So Jesus essentially said, "I don't like it, but I want what You want, Dad, even more than what I want." Because of that, the world does revolve around Jesus.

Your challenge isn't as big, but you face the same kind of choice every day. Will you choose yourself? Or will you see there's more at stake than what you feel like? Choose the option that follows God's ways.

YOUR MISSION

1. Get over yourself. Find a way to help or serve someone at school every day this week.

2. Let your brother or sister have or use or do something that you always fight to have or use or do.

3. Willingly do something to help your parents this week that you normally complain about or try to get out of doing.

YOUR DEBRIEF

- How do you act like life is only about you?

- What do you not like to do that you know God wants you to do?

- What are three actions you can choose to tell God, "Do what You want, not what I want"?

MISSION ACCOMPLISHED

What did you learn?

What do you want to remember?

Crucified!

BASED ON LUKE 23:26–52;
JOHN 19:23–28;
MATTHEW 27:32–58;
MARK 15:21–45

FOR DAYS, EXCITED JEWS FROM ALL OVER PALESTINE HAVE CROWDED INTO JERUSALEM FOR THE PASSOVER FEAST. BUT ON FRIDAY MORNING, THE CITY IS GREETED WITH STARTLING NEWS. JESUS OF NAZARETH IS GOING TO BE CRUCIFIED—FOR TREASON!

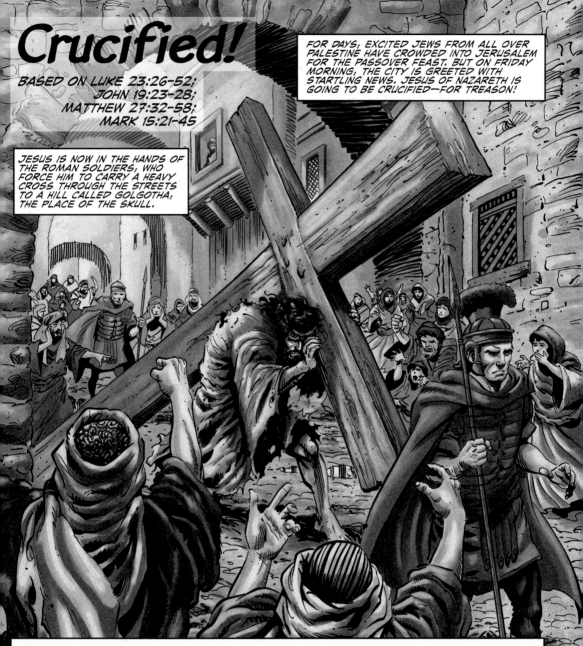

JESUS IS NOW IN THE HANDS OF THE ROMAN SOLDIERS, WHO FORCE HIM TO CARRY A HEAVY CROSS THROUGH THE STREETS TO A HILL CALLED GOLGOTHA, THE PLACE OF THE SKULL.

AS JESUS STUMBLES UNDER THE WEIGHT OF HIS CROSS, THE STREETS FILL WITH A STRANGE MIXTURE OF SPECTATORS AND MOURNERS: PRIESTS AND PHARISEES WHO DEMAND JESUS' DEATH; WOMEN WEEPING FOR THE MAN WHO FORGAVE SINS AND HEALED THE SICK; CURIOUS ONLOOKERS WHO WANT ONLY TO SEE THE CONDEMNED MAN CARRY HIS CROSS. TWO ROBBERS ARE SENTENCED TO CRUCIFIXION AS WELL.

ON THE WAY, JESUS FALLS UNDER THE WEIGHT OF THE HEAVY CROSS. TO KEEP THE UGLY PROCESSION MOVING, THE ROMAN OFFICERS SEIZE A BYSTANDER, SIMON OF CYRENE.

YOU! CARRY THE CROSS FOR HIM!

IT'S ABOUT NINE O'CLOCK IN THE MORNING WHEN JESUS AND THE TWO ROBBERS REACH GOLGOTHA. SOLDIERS NAIL THE SON OF GOD TO A CROSS BETWEEN THE ROBBERS. PILATE'S SIGN HANGS OVER HIS HEAD: "JESUS OF NAZARETH, THE KING OF THE JEWS."
FATHER, FORGIVE THEM. THEY DON'T KNOW WHAT THEY'RE DOING.

TO THE ROMAN SOLDIERS, JESUS IS JUST ANOTHER CRIMINAL. THEY NOTICE THAT JESUS HAS A NICE ROBE.

THIS ROBE IS SEAMLESS. HOW SHOULD WE DIVIDE IT?

IT'S TOO GOOD TO TEAR INTO PIECES. LET'S GAMBLE FOR IT.

AS JESUS' FRIENDS STAND WATCHING HIM SUFFER, CURIOUS CROWDS PASS BY. SOME WHO WANT HIM TO DIE TAUNT HIM.

IF YOU'RE THE KING OF THE JEWS, COME DOWN FROM THE CROSS. THEN WE'LL BELIEVE YOU.

ONE OF THE ROBBERS CRUCIFIED WITH JESUS HURLS INSULTS AT HIM TOO...

IF YOU'RE THE MESSIAH, SAVE YOURSELF AND SAVE US!

HAVE SOME RESPECT FOR GOD! WE DESERVE TO DIE FOR OUR CRIMES, BUT THIS MAN HAS DONE NOTHING WRONG.

279

LORD, REMEMBER ME WHEN YOU COME INTO YOUR KINGDOM.

TODAY YOU WILL BE WITH ME IN HEAVEN.

JESUS LOOKS DOWN AND SEES HIS MOTHER, MARY, AND HIS FRIEND JOHN AT THE FOOT OF THE CROSS, WATCHING HIS AGONY.

JOHN, TAKE CARE OF MY MOTHER.

JOHN TAKES MARY TO HIS OWN HOME AND CARES FOR HER LIKE HIS OWN MOTHER.

IT IS NOW NOON. A STRANGE SHADOW COVERS THE LAND. JESUS SUFFERS FOR THREE HOURS UNDER THE DARK SKY AND THEN CRIES OUT TO GOD ...

FATHER, I PUT MY SPIRIT IN YOUR HANDS!

JESUS DIES. AT THAT MOMENT AN EARTHQUAKE SHAKES THE GROUND.

OUTSIDE THE CITY, EVEN THE ROMAN OFFICER IN CHARGE OF THE EXECUTION IS AWED BY WHAT HAPPENED. REVERENTLY, HE LOOKS UP AT THE MAN WHO FORGAVE HIS ENEMIES.

TRULY THIS MAN WAS GOD'S SON!

A SOLDIER STABS JESUS WITH A SPEAR TO MAKE SURE HE'S DEAD. THE WITNESSES ARE FILLED WITH GRIEF. THEY SLOWLY GO BACK TO JERUSALEM.

THEY'VE NOW LOST ALL HOPE THAT JESUS WAS THE PROMISED SAVIOR WHO WOULD DELIVER THEM FROM THE ROMANS.

IN JERUSALEM, JOSEPH OF ARIMATHEA, A SECRET BELIEVER IN JESUS, GOES TO PILATE ...

MAY I HAVE THE BODY OF JESUS SO THAT WE MAY BURY IT BEFORE THE SABBATH?

YES. I'LL GIVE ORDERS TO THE OFFICER IN CHARGE.

CRUCIFIED

KEY VERSE

THEN JESUS SHOUTED, "FATHER, I ENTRUST MY SPIRIT INTO YOUR HANDS!" AND WITH THOSE WORDS HE BREATHED HIS LAST.

—Luke 23:46 NLT

X-RAY VISION

You give your best effort when you really care about something, right? You might do it to get a good grade or to win a game or to create something special or to really impress someone. But what would it take to give so much that you gave up your life?

For Jesus, it took you and me and every single person in history and the future. We mattered so much that Jesus willingly let Himself be beaten, tortured, spit on, mocked, and nailed onto a cross. It was a brutal way to die, and Jesus went through agony. He could have called down millions of angels to rescue Him. Instead, He endured the intense pain. Then when He was ready, He gave up His spirit and died.

Love kept Jesus hanging on the cross more than any nails. And love busted Him out of the grave three days later. He made the ultimate sacrifice. He finished the most heroic act in the universe. He gave everything to rescue us. And we can give everything to show our thanks. Jesus wants our lives—not for us to physically die, but to spiritually come alive. He gives us spiritual life that lasts forever. But every day we can say thanks by pointing our lives in His direction, obeying what He taught, and showing Him we love Him. We can give our all because Jesus gave us His.

YOUR MISSION

1. If you never have, give your life to Jesus by asking for His forgiveness and life.

2. Create a craft or symbol that reminds you of Jesus's sacrifice and His life in you.

3. Write a song or poem about giving Jesus everything.

YOUR DEBRIEF

- What do you think the disciples felt like as they watched Jesus die?

- How would you have saved the world?

- Are you giving God your best?

MISSION ACCOMPLISHED

What did you learn?

What do you want to remember?

SHARE THE ADVENTURE

Ask your parents if you're old enough to watch the movie *The Passion of the Christ* with them.

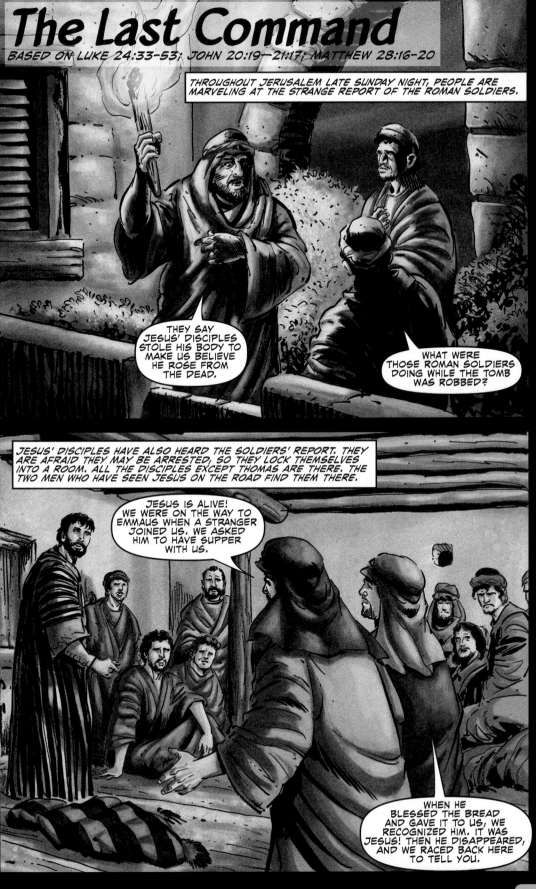

The Last Command

BASED ON LUKE 24:33-53; JOHN 20:19—21:17; MATTHEW 28:16-20

THROUGHOUT JERUSALEM LATE SUNDAY NIGHT, PEOPLE ARE MARVELING AT THE STRANGE REPORT OF THE ROMAN SOLDIERS.

THEY SAY JESUS' DISCIPLES STOLE HIS BODY TO MAKE US BELIEVE HE ROSE FROM THE DEAD.

WHAT WERE THOSE ROMAN SOLDIERS DOING WHILE THE TOMB WAS ROBBED?

JESUS' DISCIPLES HAVE ALSO HEARD THE SOLDIERS' REPORT. THEY ARE AFRAID THEY MAY BE ARRESTED, SO THEY LOCK THEMSELVES INTO A ROOM. ALL THE DISCIPLES EXCEPT THOMAS ARE THERE. THE TWO MEN WHO HAVE SEEN JESUS ON THE ROAD FIND THEM THERE.

JESUS IS ALIVE! WE WERE ON THE WAY TO EMMAUS WHEN A STRANGER JOINED US. WE ASKED HIM TO HAVE SUPPER WITH US.

WHEN HE BLESSED THE BREAD AND GAVE IT TO US, WE RECOGNIZED HIM. IT WAS JESUS! THEN HE DISAPPEARED, AND WE RACED BACK HERE TO TELL YOU.

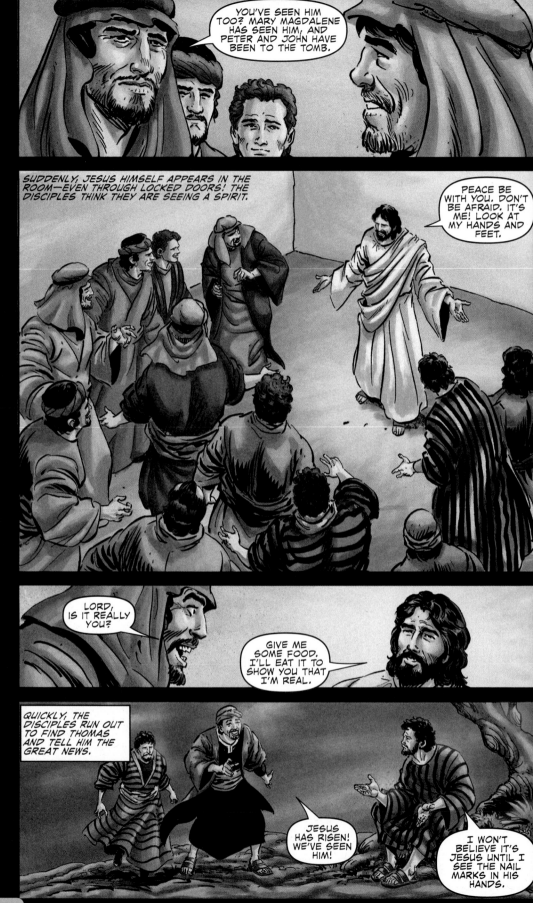

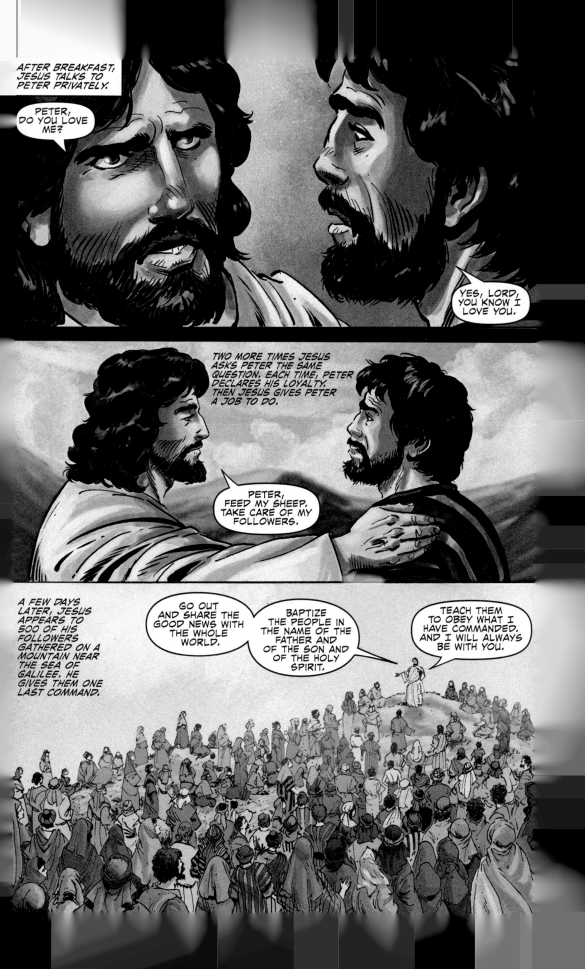

JESUS EXPLAINS HOW HE HAS COMPLETED GOD'S WORK. HE IS THE SAVIOR OF THE WORLD. NOW IT'S THEIR TURN TO CARRY ON GOD'S WORK. JESUS TELLS THEM TO WAIT IN JERUSALEM FOR THE HOLY SPIRIT TO COME.

THEN, WITH HIS FOLLOWERS GATHERED AROUND HIM ON THE MOUNT OF OLIVES NEAR BETHANY, JESUS ASCENDS INTO HEAVEN.

THE LAST COMMAND

KEY VERSE

SO GO AND MAKE FOLLOWERS OF ALL PEOPLE IN THE WORLD. BAPTIZE THEM IN THE NAME OF THE FATHER AND THE SON AND THE HOLY SPIRIT. TEACH THEM TO OBEY EVERYTHING THAT I HAVE TAUGHT YOU, AND I WILL BE WITH YOU ALWAYS, EVEN UNTIL THE END OF THIS AGE.

—Matthew 28:19–20 NCV

X-RAY VISION

Every hero needs a cause. Every agent needs a mission. Every good character in every good story needs a purpose. You've got yours.

Jesus came back to life and came back to earth again. That's when He gave His followers their mission. He had done His part of God's big plan so far. Now God was putting the work in human hands. It was time for Jesus's followers to live out all He'd taught them. It was time for them to spread the word and teach other people about all Jesus had done and about the life He offered.

That's our mission too: show other people and teach them what following Jesus looks like. You like sharing good news, right? The life God has given is the greatest thing to happen to us. There are no magic words; we just need what comes out naturally about what God does in our lives. We can use our words and our actions. And God promises that we've always got the help of His Spirit. We're fully equipped. Time to get going!

YOUR MISSION

1. Invite a friend to church or a church event this week.

2. Ask a friend this week what he or she believes and talk about what Jesus means to you.

3. Pick an action that shows love in a way that makes people say, "Wow!"

YOUR DEBRIEF

- Is it hard to talk to your friends about Jesus?

- Do your actions point to God?

- Who do you need to talk to about Jesus?

MISSION ACCOMPLISHED

What did you learn?

What do you want to remember?

SHARE THE ADVENTURE

Talk to your parents or youth leader about good ways to share Jesus.

NOTHING SAYS GOD LOVES YOU
LIKE ... (WRITE OR DRAW)

Tongues of Fire!

BASED ON ACTS 2

EARLY ON THE DAY OF PENTECOST, 120 FOLLOWERS OF JESUS GATHER TO PRAY. SUDDENLY A SOUND LIKE A MIGHTY RUSHING WIND ROARS THROUGH THE ROOM AND FILLS THE WHOLE HOUSE. THEN, TONGUES OF FIRE SETTLE ON THEM.

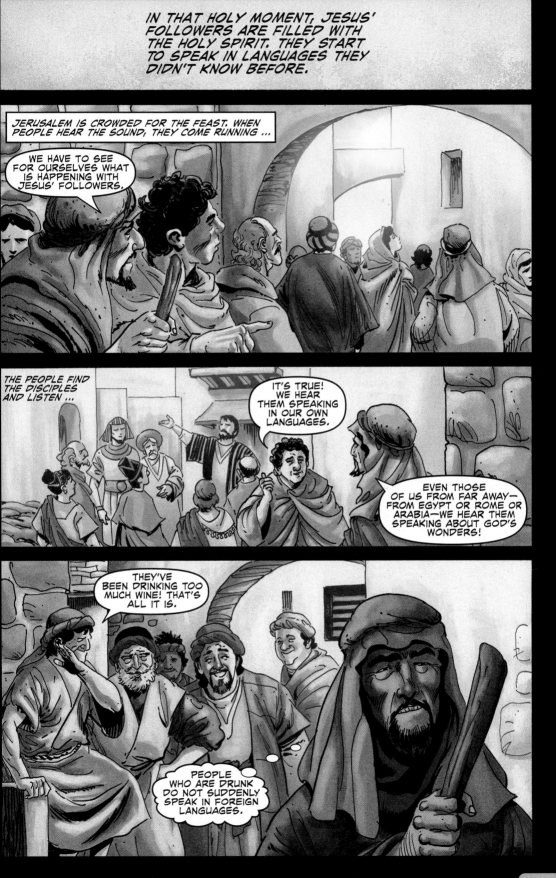

IN THAT HOLY MOMENT, JESUS' FOLLOWERS ARE FILLED WITH THE HOLY SPIRIT. THEY START TO SPEAK IN LANGUAGES THEY DIDN'T KNOW BEFORE.

JERUSALEM IS CROWDED FOR THE FEAST. WHEN PEOPLE HEAR THE SOUND, THEY COME RUNNING ...

WE HAVE TO SEE FOR OURSELVES WHAT IS HAPPENING WITH JESUS' FOLLOWERS.

THE PEOPLE FIND THE DISCIPLES AND LISTEN ...

IT'S TRUE! WE HEAR THEM SPEAKING IN OUR OWN LANGUAGES.

EVEN THOSE OF US FROM FAR AWAY— FROM EGYPT OR ROME OR ARABIA—WE HEAR THEM SPEAKING ABOUT GOD'S WONDERS!

THEY'VE BEEN DRINKING TOO MUCH WINE! THAT'S ALL IT IS.

PEOPLE WHO ARE DRUNK DO NOT SUDDENLY SPEAK IN FOREIGN LANGUAGES.

PETER SPEAKS OUT FOR ALL THE DISCIPLES.

WE ARE NOT DRUNK! WE ARE FILLED WITH THE HOLY SPIRIT. AS THE PROPHET JOEL PREDICTED, YOU CRUCIFIED JESUS, THE CHOSEN ONE OF GOD. BUT GOD RAISED HIM FROM THE DEAD, AND WE ARE WITNESSES TO HIS RESURRECTION.

PETER'S WORDS CUT DEEP INTO THE HEARTS OF THE PEOPLE. THEY REMEMBER HOW THEY HAD DEMANDED JESUS' CRUCIFIXION ONLY A FEW WEEKS EARLIER.

STOP YOUR SINNING WAYS! BE BAPTIZED IN THE NAME OF JESUS. THEN YOU WILL RECEIVE GOD'S HOLY SPIRIT FOR YOURSELVES.

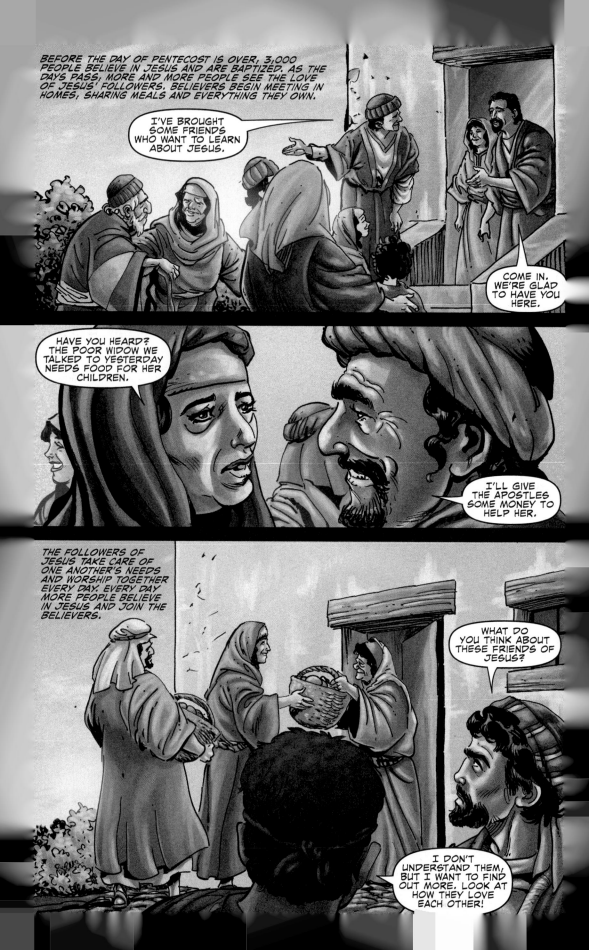

TONGUES OF FIRE!

KEY VERSE

ALL THE BELIEVERS WERE TOGETHER AND SHARED EVERYTHING. THEY WOULD SELL THEIR LAND AND THE THINGS THEY OWNED AND THEN DIVIDE THE MONEY AND GIVE IT TO ANYONE WHO NEEDED IT. THE BELIEVERS MET TOGETHER IN THE TEMPLE EVERY DAY. THEY ATE TOGETHER IN THEIR HOMES, HAPPY TO SHARE THEIR FOOD WITH JOYFUL HEARTS. THEY PRAISED GOD AND WERE LIKED BY ALL THE PEOPLE. EVERY DAY THE LORD ADDED THOSE WHO WERE BEING SAVED TO THE GROUP OF BELIEVERS.

—Acts 2:44–47 NCV

X-RAY VISION

Nobody likes a know-it-all. Do you have one in your class? You know, that kid who tries to answer every question without giving anyone else a chance. The one who can't just answer the question simply but has to go on and on like a human Wikipedia. Being smart is a great thing—it's a gift from God. But trying to act like you know everything in the world just turns people off.

The same is true when it comes to knowing about God. Running your mouth to prove how much you know about the Bible just makes you seem arrogant. It doesn't draw people toward God; it pushes them away.

The believers in the early church showed that following Jesus is about living a different way. With the Holy Spirit's help, they shared all they had with each other: money, food, stuff. They looked out for other people. They talked about Jesus, and they backed up their words by putting love into action. Guess what? People noticed. They saw that Jesus's followers had something different, and they wanted to find out what it was.

We should try to have the same attitude: paying attention to other people, including them, helping them. Share encouragement, kindness, and life with people around you. Others will notice—they'll see Jesus in you.

YOUR MISSION

1. Try to get to know someone this week who you usually ignore.

2. Let someone else go first this week, maybe in line, during a game, or at home.

3. When people begin making fun of a kid this week, point out a good trait that kid has and ask them to stop mocking.

YOUR DEBRIEF

- How often do you think about helping other people?

- Would most people describe you as proud or humble?

- How can your life look different than someone's who doesn't follow Jesus?

MISSION ACCOMPLISHED

What did you learn?

What do you want to remember?

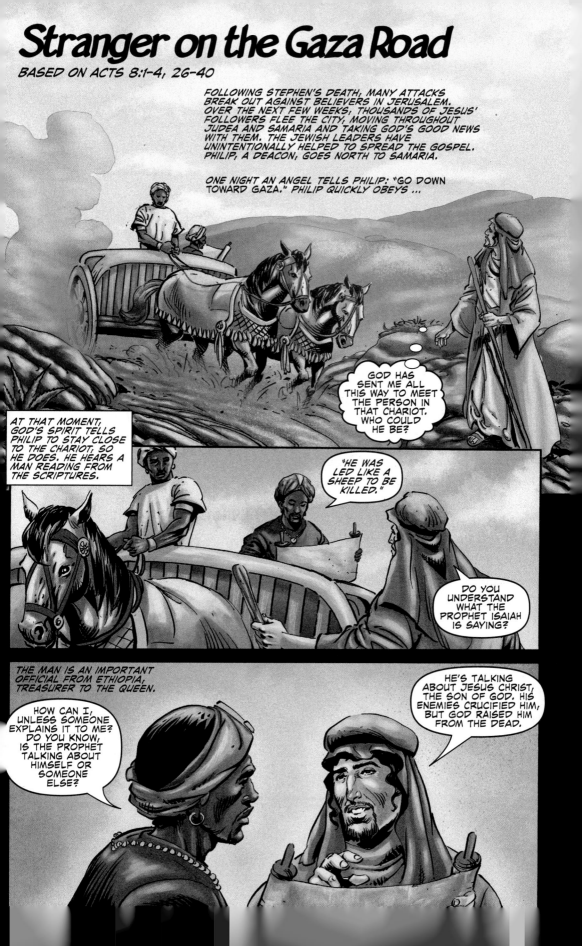

STRANGER ON THE GAZA ROAD

KEY VERSE

SO HE STARTED OUT, AND HE MET THE TREASURER OF ETHIOPIA, A EUNUCH OF GREAT AUTHORITY UNDER THE KANDAKE, THE QUEEN OF ETHIOPIA.

—Acts 8:27 NLT

X-RAY VISION

You know people are different. Some of your friends are tall and some short. They like different foods and activities. Some are loud, and some are quiet. Some are bold, and some are shy. They have different-colored hair and eyes. But what about their skin?

Philip got sent on a special mission by an angel. God sent him out in the desert to meet a man from Ethiopia who had questions about God. Philip told him about Jesus, and the man took the word to his queen and people. The Jewish Christians were already spreading out across Israel and taking God's message with them. But this story shows us that God clearly wanted His message to go to Africa, too. God wanted His love to go to people of every color and country. He still does.

Our country has a painful past between black and white people. Things are much better, but many of our different-colored people—even Christians—still keep pretty separate. What about you? You may not feel like you're prejudiced, but do you live like it? Don't avoid people who look different from you. Get to know them. Discover their cool cultures. Taste their unusual foods. Look at them and love them like God does—as people made in His image.

YOUR MISSION

1. Introduce yourself and make a friend this week who doesn't look like you.

2. Ask your parents to take you to a cultural festival, maybe Greek, Latino, or Native American.

3. When someone tells mean jokes about another race, tell them it's not funny and walk away.

YOUR DEBRIEF

- How colorful are your friends?

- What do you think about people of different races?

- Who have you avoided because they seem different?

MISSION ACCOMPLISHED

What did you learn?

What do you want to remember?

SHARE THE ADVENTURE

Get a pen pal in a different country. With your parents, check out kidzhelpingkids.org or clubhousemagazine.com.

The Next Journey

BASED ON ACTS 15:36—16:19

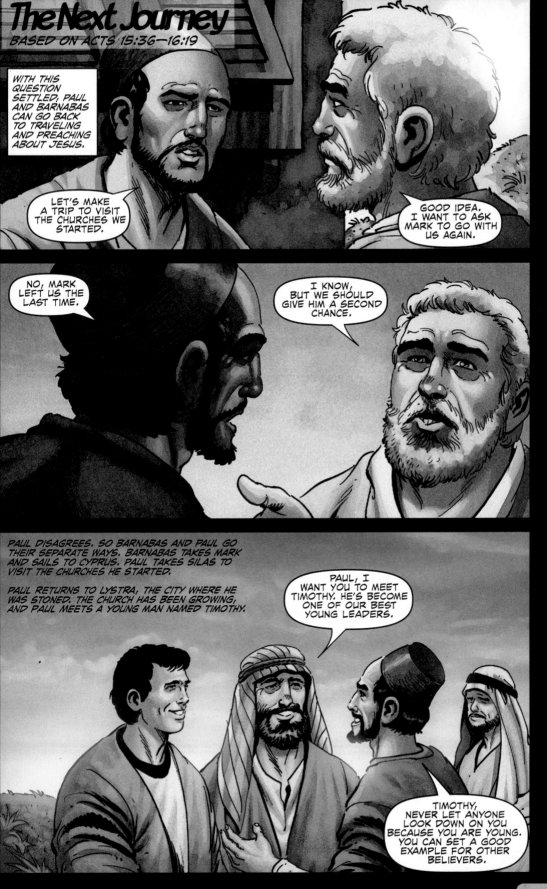

WITH THIS QUESTION SETTLED, PAUL AND BARNABAS CAN GO BACK TO TRAVELING AND PREACHING ABOUT JESUS.

LET'S MAKE A TRIP TO VISIT THE CHURCHES WE STARTED.

GOOD IDEA. I WANT TO ASK MARK TO GO WITH US AGAIN.

NO, MARK LEFT US THE LAST TIME.

I KNOW, BUT WE SHOULD GIVE HIM A SECOND CHANCE.

PAUL DISAGREES. SO BARNABAS AND PAUL GO THEIR SEPARATE WAYS. BARNABAS TAKES MARK AND SAILS TO CYPRUS. PAUL TAKES SILAS TO VISIT THE CHURCHES HE STARTED.

PAUL RETURNS TO LYSTRA, THE CITY WHERE HE WAS STONED. THE CHURCH HAS BEEN GROWING, AND PAUL MEETS A YOUNG MAN NAMED TIMOTHY.

PAUL, I WANT YOU TO MEET TIMOTHY. HE'S BECOME ONE OF OUR BEST YOUNG LEADERS.

TIMOTHY, NEVER LET ANYONE LOOK DOWN ON YOU BECAUSE YOU ARE YOUNG. YOU CAN SET A GOOD EXAMPLE FOR OTHER BELIEVERS.

TIMOTHY EAGERLY JOINS PAUL ON HIS JOURNEY. SOON THE THREE TRAVELERS ARE ON THEIR WAY. GOD TELLS THEM NOT TO FOLLOW THE ROAD TO EPHESUS. INSTEAD THEY GO NORTH AND WEST UNTIL THEY REACH TROAS ON THE AEGEAN SEA.

IN TROAS, PAUL MEETS ANOTHER NEW FRIEND ...

DR. LUKE! THE LORD MUST HAVE LED YOU TO JOIN US HERE.

I CAN'T WAIT TO TRAVEL WITH YOU AND SEE WHAT GOD WILL DO.

AS THE FOUR MISSIONARIES WALK THE STREETS OF THE GREAT SEAPORT ...

I WONDER WHERE GOD WANTS US TO GO NEXT?

THE HOLY SPIRIT WILL TELL US SOON.

AND I'LL RECORD ALL OUR ADVENTURES IN MY JOURNAL!

SOON ALL THE MEMBERS OF LYDIA'S HOUSEHOLD ARE BAPTIZED. LYDIA INVITES THE MISSIONARIES TO MAKE HER HOME THEIR HEADQUARTERS WHILE THEY ARE IN PHILIPPI.

THE ROMANS LOVE PURPLE. I SELL MOST OF MY CLOTH TO THEM.

AS YOU SELL TO THEM, TELL THEM ABOUT JESUS.

EVERY DAY AS PAUL AND SILAS WALK THROUGH THE STREETS OF PHILIPPI, THEY SEE A SAD SIGHT...

THE POOR GIRL IS UNDER THE INFLUENCE OF AN EVIL SPIRIT. HER MASTERS EARN LOTS OF MONEY USING HER AS A FORTUNE-TELLER.

FINALLY, ONE DAY...

YOU SERVE THE MOST HIGH GOD!

IN CHRIST'S NAME, COME OUT OF HER!

LOOK! SHE CAN'T TELL FORTUNES ANYMORE. OUR BUSINESS IS RUINED.

WHOEVER THAT MAN IS, HE'LL PAY FOR THIS. HE HAD NO RIGHT TO MEDDLE WITH OUR AFFAIRS.

KEY VERSE

DON'T LET ANYONE THINK LESS OF YOU BECAUSE YOU ARE YOUNG. BE AN EXAMPLE TO ALL BELIEVERS IN WHAT YOU SAY, IN THE WAY YOU LIVE, IN YOUR LOVE, YOUR FAITH, AND YOUR PURITY.

—1 Timothy 4:12 NLT

X-RAY VISION

Who me? I'm just a kid!

Uh—so? Being a kid's not an excuse. It's a rallying cry! Say it loud—"I'm a kid, and I'm proud!" Kids and teens have sailed around the world, climbed the highest mountains, designed apps and websites, and started organizations to fight hunger, poverty, disease, and slavery.

How? They heard about a need or set a goal and decided to do something about it. Most started with a small step. They prayed for God's help, and they got a hand from parents, friends, and teachers. Then more people got impressed and joined the cause—because they thought, *If a kid can do that, so can I.*

That's the kind of example Paul was telling Timothy to be—and the kind you can be. Does that mean you have to start your own movement? No. (But don't let your age hold you back.) You can make a difference and be an example right where you are at school, home, and in your neighborhood. Reach out and love other people. Look for little ways to help them every day. Treat kids and adults with respect. Live for God. Your age and your action can inspire many more people.

YOUR MISSION

1. Go for it. What have you wanted to try? Ask your parents for help and get started.

2. Set three goals: one to accomplish this week, one for this month, and one for this year.

3. Be an example for your brothers and sisters by doing your chores without complaining.

YOUR DEBRIEF

• What are some benefits of being a kid?

• What can you learn now to help you later in life?

• If you could change one thing about the world, what would it be?

MISSION ACCOMPLISHED

What did you learn?

What do you want to remember?

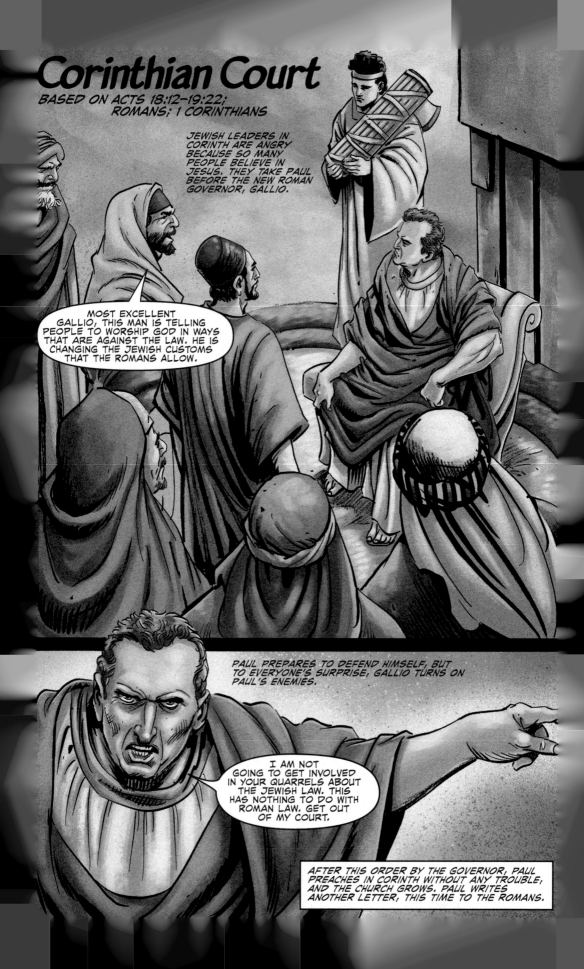

Black Sea

PHILIPPI
NEAPOLIS
THESSALONICA
BEREA
TROAS

Aegean Sea

ASIA

ANTIOCH
ICONIUM
TARSUS

ATHENS
EPHESUS
Galatia
LYSTRA
DERBE
ANTIOCH
SELEUCIA

CORINTH
MILETUS

Mediterranean Sea

CYPRUS

SIDON
TYRE

CAESAREA
JERUSALEM

PAUL'S LETTER TO THE ROMANS ...

Everybody—Roman or Greek, Jew or Gentile—needs God, because everybody has sinned and fallen short of God's perfection. But we are no longer punished by the law, because Christ Jesus gave us the law of the Spirit of life, which sets us free from the law of sin and death.

PAUL VISITS JERUSALEM AND ANTIOCH. THEN HE BEGINS HIS THIRD MISSIONARY JOURNEY. IN EPHESUS, HE SEES THE GREAT TEMPLE OF THE GODDESS ARTEMIS.

LIKE THE PEOPLE OF ATHENS, THE EPHESIANS WORSHIP A GODDESS MADE WITH THEIR OWN HANDS. GOD, HELP ME TO TEACH THEM THE TRUTH.

THE PEOPLE OF EPHESUS LISTEN TO PAUL AND SEE THAT WHAT HE SAYS IS TRUE AND THAT THEIR MAGICIANS ARE FAKES. MANY PEOPLE BELIEVE IN JESUS AND BURN THEIR BOOKS OF MAGIC.

THOSE SCROLLS ARE WORTH A FORTUNE!

YES, BUT THEIR NEW LIFE IN JESUS IS WORTH EVEN MORE!

PAUL IS STILL REJOICING ABOUT THE GROWTH OF THE CHURCH IN EPHESUS WHEN NEWS COMES FROM CORINTH ...

THE CHURCH IN CORINTH IS HAVING ALL KINDS OF TROUBLE. THE MEMBERS ARE TAKING SIDES AGAINST EACH OTHER. SOME OF THEM SAY *YOU* ARE THE HEAD OF THE CHURCH. OTHERS SAY APOLLOS IS THE BEST PREACHER. OTHERS SAY PETER IS THE REAL LEADER.

SO PAUL SENDS A LETTER TO THE CHURCH AT CORINTH.

PAUL'S FIRST LETTER TO THE CORINTHIANS ...

I beg of you, my brothers, do not quarrel and divide the Church. The Church has only one head—Christ, who died on the cross.

Keep yourselves pure, because your body is a temple of the Holy Spirit. So whatever you do with your body, eating or drinking or anything else, do it to honor God.

We've all been given different gifts of the Spirit so that we can build up the church in different ways. But even if I had all the gifts possible—if I knew everything and could speak the language of angels—it would mean nothing if I didn't have love.

KEY VERSE

THREE THINGS WILL LAST FOREVER—FAITH, HOPE, AND LOVE—AND THE GREATEST OF THESE IS LOVE.

—1 Corinthians 13:13 NLT

X-RAY VISION

You've probably got cliques in your school. Cliques are little groups of people who stick together and exclude others. They call people names or ignore others. They might be the mean girls or the jocks. They act like no one's as cool as they are and you'd better not forget it.

Usually there's more than one clique, and the different groups trade insults and spread rumors. They snip and snap and put down the other side to try to make their side seem more important.

Sound familiar? Would you believe it happened in the Bible, too? That's why Paul wrote 1 Corinthians. The people were fighting about who was better and more spiritual. Know what Paul's answer was? Well, the whole letter was his answer, but it all came down to this: love.

Not mushy-gushy, love-song-on-the-radio counterfeit love but the real thing. Love that's patient, kind, hopeful, humble, forgiving, and giving instead of taking—God's love. That's the kind of love we need to offer other people. That's the kind of love that breaks down differences, builds people up, and erases cliques. That's the kind of love that lasts forever.

YOUR MISSION

1. Who doesn't like you? Choose one way to show love and kindness to him or her.

2. Break the clique. Talk and play with kids in other groups.

3. Put love in action. Offer to help your mom or dad. Or do a chore for your brother or sister.

YOUR DEBRIEF

• How is God's love different from love-song love?

• Can you love someone who hates you? How?

• How does love lead you to forgive?

MISSION ACCOMPLISHED

What did you learn?

What do you want to remember?

LOVE ...

HISTORICAL BACKGROUND ...

IN THE YEAR 64, NERO, THE CRUEL EMPEROR OF ROME, HAS MANY ENEMIES AMONG HIS OWN PEOPLE. RUMORS SPREAD ABOUT PLOTS ON HIS LIFE. SUDDENLY A FIRE SWEEPS ACROSS THE CITY AND RAGES FOR NINE DAYS. GREAT SECTIONS OF THE CITY BURN TO THE GROUND, DRIVING THOUSANDS OF PEOPLE FROM THEIR HOMES.

Fight the Good Fight

BASED ON TITUS; 2 TIMOTHY

FROM ROME, PAUL WRITES HIS FINAL LETTERS ...

PAUL'S LETTER TO TITUS ...

We followers of Christ must be good examples to the world. Be honest and serious, careful about what you say. That way, your enemies will be embarrassed, because no one will believe anything bad about you.

PAUL'S SECOND LETTER TO TIMOTHY ...

Be strong, like a soldier for Christ. Remember the truth you learned from me and the Scriptures. Keep preaching it, even though the time will come when people don't want to hear the truth. Follow Scripture, because it is all inspired by God, and it equips us to do good.

PAUL'S CASE COMES TO TRIAL. GUARDS MARCH HIM INTO THE COURT OF NERO ...

 # FIGHT THE GOOD FIGHT

 ## KEY VERSE

I HAVE FOUGHT THE GOOD FIGHT, I HAVE FINISHED THE RACE, AND I HAVE REMAINED FAITHFUL.

—2 Timothy 4:7 NLT

 ## X-RAY VISION

Does Sunday school make you sleepy? Think the Bible is boring? Do you ever feel like following Jesus is for wimps and goody-goodys? Does it feel like a long list of rules? Then listen to this: *Fight the good fight. Run the race. Win the prize. Train my body.* Those aren't words of sleepy sermons. Those are words of champions. Those are phrases of action. And those are all from the Bible.

They were all written by the apostle Paul. When it came to giving everything he had to serve Jesus, Paul was hard-core. He lived his faith as a heroic adventure all the way to the end. He gave everything he had to obey God and to tell other people about Jesus. He was no wimp. He endured beatings and prison and a shipwreck. And eventually following Jesus cost him his life. But even when Paul knew he was going to die he said, "I have fought the good fight."

You can live your faith like an adventure too—all the way to the end. You can give God everything you've got just like you do when you're going for the winning basket or goal or finish line. There might be days you lose or times you feel like your spirit gets beat up. You might feel lost in the wilderness sometimes, but that's when God can show up and save the day. Adventure isn't always safe, and neither is faith. That's what keeps it from being boring.

Tell God you're all in, all the way to the end. Give Him everything you've got. And let Him lead you on a great adventure.

YOUR MISSION

1. Practice your faith like your sport. Each day this week focus on one move: maybe obeying your parents or giving kind words to the outcast at school.

2. Fight temptation by learning and saying a verse, such as 1 Corinthians 10:13, Psalm 119:11, or James 4:7.

3. Create an adventure photo story of your faith. Look for pictures in magazines or take your own that represent the way you want to live for God.

YOUR DEBRIEF

• How do you view your faith: boring or adventurous?

• What big thing would you like to accomplish for God?

• Are you giving God everything you've got or holding back your best?

MISSION ACCOMPLISHED

What did you learn?

What do you want to remember?

The Final Letters

THE LAST EIGHT LETTERS OF THE NEW TESTAMENT, HEBREWS THROUGH JUDE, ARE MESSAGES THAT JESUS' DISCIPLES WROTE TO GIVE ADVICE, COURAGE, AND COMFORT TO THE EARLY CHRISTIANS.

THE BOOK OF HEBREWS

THE LETTER TO THE HEBREWS WAS WRITTEN WHEN JEWISH CHRISTIANS WERE BEING PRESSURED TO GIVE UP THEIR FAITH IN JESUS AND RETURN TO THEIR JEWISH TRADITIONS. THEY ASKED THEMSELVES, WHICH IS RIGHT: FAITH IN JESUS OR FAITH IN THE RELIGION OF ABRAHAM, MOSES, AND DAVID?

In the past, God spoke to our people through the prophets. But in these last days, He has spoken to us through His Son. All the faith heroes of the past looked forward to Jesus, even though He didn't come during their lifetime. Now that Jesus has come, throw away your sin and run the good race, because Jesus is waiting for us at the finish line. While you're running, remember what God said to us: "I will never leave you."

THE BOOK OF JAMES

THE LEADER OF THE CHURCH IN JERUSALEM, JAMES, THE BROTHER OF JESUS, WROTE A LETTER TO ENCOURAGE CHRISTIANS TO LIVE IN WAYS THAT SHOW THEIR FAITH.

Faith is meaningless unless you do something with it. Take care of the helpless. Ask God for wisdom, and keep your lives pure from the muck that surrounds you. Then your prayers will be powerful and change the world.

THE BOOK OF 1 PETER

PETER WROTE TO ENCOURAGE THE CHRISTIANS WHO WERE BEING PERSECUTED. LIKE PAUL, HE WAS ALSO EXECUTED BY THE ROMANS.

Face your hardships bravely. God chose you to be His royal priesthood and His holy nation. Even though the devil prowls like a lion to destroy you, stand firm.

THE BOOK OF 2 PETER

Don't be deceived by those who spread lies to mislead you. They'll get what they deserve when Christ returns. Don't be impatient waiting for Christ; God is taking His time so that people have a chance to repent.

JOHN, THE APOSTLE JESUS LOVED, WAS THE ONLY DISCIPLE WHO WAS NOT EXECUTED FOR HIS FAITH. HE LIVED TO AN OLD AGE, EXILED TO A GREEK ISLAND IN THE AEGEAN SEA. HE WROTE THREE LETTERS ABOUT GOD'S NATURE AND HOW CHRISTIANS SHOULD TREAT EACH OTHER.

THE BOOK OF 1 JOHN

God is pure light. Anyone who denies the truth of Jesus walks in darkness. If we pretend we've never sinned, then we're only lying to ourselves. But if we admit our sins, God forgives us and cleans us. My friends, make sure you show love to each other. Why? Because love comes from God, and by loving others we know God even better.

THE BOOK OF 2 JOHN

I am glad to hear that you are obeying God's commands and loving one another. Beware of enemies of the truth. These people say that Christ was just a man. Don't let them hang around you and do not invite them home! I have much to say, but not with pen and ink—I cannot wait to talk with all of you face-to-face.

THE BOOK OF 3 JOHN

You are doing right by receiving Christians into your home, especially traveling preachers. Your kindness helps in their work. Don't copy evil. Imitate what is good. Never let anyone stop you from doing good things. Peace to you.

JUDE WAS ANOTHER BROTHER OF JESUS WHO WROTE TO DEFEND TRUTH AGAINST FALSE TEACHERS.

THE BOOK OF JUDE

Dear friends, you must defend our Christian truth. Build up your faith, and pray with the help of the Holy Spirit. Have mercy for those who doubt, so you can save them from the fire of fear.

SO YOU SEE, FAITH BY ITSELF ISN'T ENOUGH. UNLESS IT PRODUCES GOOD DEEDS, IT IS DEAD AND USELESS.

—James 2:17 NLT

A car won't go without gas. A glove does nothing without a hand. A sailboat needs the wind to go anywhere. An instrument is worthless without a musician. Electricity won't spark till you connect both poles. Your body is dead without breath.

Your faith is the same without actions: dead. The two work together. They need each other. They motivate each other. They power each other. They prove each other and keep each other going.

If your words say you follow Jesus, your actions should prove it. If you feel like you love Jesus, your obedience shows that you really care about Him and about what He cares about. If you say God is most important to you, your time and energy serving Him show your priorities.

Belief happens in your head and heart. Action goes on with your hands. Bringing the two together keeps it all alive. Be like a scientist testing her theories. Be like a player practicing his skills. Be like a performer when the lights go on. Take all you think and show that you know. Live your faith in God by taking a step out the door. Spark your spirit by joining your faith and action wires. Show your love for God by showing love to other people.

YOUR MISSION

1. Go mow, rake, weed, or shovel snow for a neighbor, especially an older one, who needs help.

2. Give some money to a ministry that helps people in need.

3. In your regular Bible, read the full text of one of the final letters listed in *The Action Bible*. They're pretty short.

YOUR DEBRIEF

- Is your faith thriving or is it on life support?

- What makes God feel real to you?

- How do you show what you believe?

MISSION ACCOMPLISHED

What did you learn?

What do you want to remember?

The Final Days
BASED ON REVELATION

MANY YEARS HAVE PASSED SINCE JESUS CAME BACK TO LIFE AND ROSE UP TO HEAVEN. PAUL AND PETER HAVE DIED DOING THE WORK OF THE LORD. JOHN—JESUS' BELOVED DISCIPLE AND FRIEND—IS THE LAST APOSTLE LEFT. JESUS VISITS HIM IN ONE FINAL VISION, WHERE HE REVEALS WHAT WILL HAPPEN AT THE END OF TIME.

IN THE END DAYS, FOUR HORSEMEN WILL RIDE FORTH. FIRST A CONQUEROR, ON A WHITE HORSE. THEN WAR, RIDING ON A RED HORSE. THIRD WILL COME FAMINE, ON A BLACK HORSE. AND FINALLY, DEATH WILL COME FORTH ON A PALE HORSE, WITH HELL FOLLOWING CLOSE BEHIND HIM.

DO NOT BE AFRAID. I AM THE FIRST AND THE LAST, WHO LIVES FOREVER AND EVER. I HOLD THE KEYS TO DEATH AND HELL.

AS THE FOUR HORSEMEN RIDE THROUGH THE SKY, AN EARTHQUAKE SHAKES THE LAND. THE SUN TURNS BLACK, THE MOON TURNS RED, AND THE STARS IN THE SKY FALL TO THE EARTH. MANY PEOPLE ARE KILLED BY WAR, PLAGUES, FAMINE—EVEN BY WILD ANIMALS!

AFTER THE FOUR HORSEMEN FINISH BRINGING THEIR SUFFERING TO THE EARTH, THE DEVIL WILL COME IN THE FORM OF A RED DRAGON. HE WILL PERFORM MIRACLES, RAINING FIRE DOWN FROM HEAVEN. THE PEOPLE WILL BE DECEIVED AND WORSHIP HIM.

THROUGH THE PROPHECY IN REVELATION, JESUS GIVES JOHN A MESSAGE FOR THE SEVEN CHURCHES IN ASIA. SOME PEOPLE AT THOSE CHURCHES HAVE BEEN FAITHFUL FOLLOWERS. SOME HAVE TURNED AWAY FROM JESUS BECAUSE IT WAS TOO HARD TO FOLLOW HIM. AND SOME JUST WANT THINGS TO BE EASY. JESUS' WORDS TO THESE CHURCHES ARE STILL RELEVANT TO US TODAY.

"I KNOW WHAT YOU'VE BEEN DOING, AND IT'S NEITHER HOT NOR COLD. I WISH YOU'D BE ONE OR THE OTHER.

BECAUSE YOU ARE LUKEWARM—NEITHER COLD NOR HOT—I WILL SPIT YOU OUT OF MY MOUTH.

YOU THINK YOU ARE RICH, BUT YOU HAVE NO IDEA HOW POOR, BLIND, AND NAKED YOU ARE.

TAKE THE WEALTH I GIVE YOU, AND YOU WILL TRULY BE RICH. MY WHITE CLOTHES WILL COVER YOUR SINFUL NAKEDNESS. THE SALVE I GIVE YOU WILL LET YOU SEE!"

"HERE I AM! I'M STANDING AT THE DOOR AND KNOCKING. ANYONE WHO HEARS MY VOICE AND OPENS THE DOOR WILL SHARE MY FOOD AND MY THRONE IN HEAVEN!

JOHN'S VISION ENDS THE BIBLE, THE GREATEST STORY EVER TOLD.

JESUS STANDS AT THE DOOR AND KNOCKS. WILL YOU LET HIM IN?

KEY VERSE

> *I HEARD A LOUD SHOUT FROM THE THRONE, SAYING, "LOOK, GOD'S HOME IS NOW AMONG HIS PEOPLE! HE WILL LIVE WITH THEM, AND THEY WILL BE HIS PEOPLE. GOD HIMSELF WILL BE WITH THEM. HE WILL WIPE EVERY TEAR FROM THEIR EYES, AND THERE WILL BE NO MORE DEATH OR SORROW OR CRYING OR PAIN. ALL THESE THINGS ARE GONE FOREVER."*
>
> —Revelation 21:3–4 NLT

X-RAY VISION

Do you ever cheat by skipping ahead and reading the end of a novel? I know, sometimes the suspense is too much. You just can't help it. But then it changes the way you read the story because you know what happens. You're not afraid for the characters. You know they'll be okay. You know the hero is going to win.

That's why you've got to check out Revelation. Weird book? *Kind of.* Confusing? *It can be.* But don't complicate it. It sounds like the fantasy novel of the Bible, filled with crazy creatures and otherworldly events. It's actually kind of cool. And it gives us the end of the story.

God wins! We win. You win. It's the grand finale of God's big story. It's Jesus's big return in full power. It's God saying, "Enough of all this evil!" It's putting everything together with the perfection God always wanted—and us getting to enjoy it forever.

That ending hasn't happened yet, but it makes all the difference for us now. Get it? It's going to be okay. There's more that happens after life on this earth. Yes, your problems and pains will hurt for a while. Your mistakes will still cost you. You'll lose some battles along the way, but eventually you'll win the war. God will heal you completely. You can live without the fear. You can get answers to all your questions. You can be free from worrying about what other people think. You can keep going when you don't know the way. You can do it! Live like you win—because with Jesus, you do!

YOUR MISSION

1. Remind yourself every morning this week, "I win!" Then live like it.

2. Draw your battle gear. Check out Ephesians 6:10–18 for some pointers.

3. Act out part or all of Revelation with friends or using dolls and action figures.

YOUR DEBRIEF

- What would you do if you knew you couldn't fail?

- Do you feel like a winner?

- What do you want to accomplish with God's strength?

MISSION ACCOMPLISHED

What did you learn?

What do you want to remember?

BIG PICTURE PAGE

HERE'S WHAT I'M GOING TO DO NEXT YEAR:

THE END AND
THE BEGINNING

Congratulations! You made it. You stuck with this book for an entire year. That's a great accomplishment. You can feel proud about it. I'm sure your parents do. You dove into the Bible and put it into action. You finished an adventure. Way to go!

But it's only the beginning. You've reached the end of this book. And it's also the beginning of a new year and the rest of your journey with God. Adventuring with Him is more than one book. It's a way to live a lifetime. Keep going for it! Keep going with God!

You've taken some challenging missions this year. You've lived out some cool God-sized adventures. You've hopefully seen some superhero feats. You've put the faith you believe into the life you live every day. You've grown and changed a lot in the past fifty-two weeks. So don't stop now.

Build on the good habits you formed this year. Look back at your drawings and notes. Keep practicing them. Keep going for your goals. Keep diving into God's Word and living with Him in everything you do. Now you can read the entire *Action Bible* and look for your own action missions in the rest of those stories.

As you keep going, God will always go with you. You'll face new challenges—that's part of life. But they keep the adventure exciting. Don't give up! Always look to God! He'll pick you up when you fall. He'll bring you help from people around you. He'll always give you what you need for your mission. Keep the action going, and stay adventurous at heart!

Now, time to go out with one last mission: fill out this last Big Picture Page …

THE LAST
BIG PICTURE PAGE

LOOK BACK THROUGH THIS WHOLE BOOK ...

MY FAVORITE MISSION:

MY HARDEST MISSION:

BIGGEST THINGS I LEARNED:

WAYS I SAW GOD IN MY LIFE:

GOOD HABITS I MADE:

BAD HABITS I BROKE:

MY GOALS FOR NEXT YEAR:

FRIENDS I CAN GIVE A COPY OF THIS BOOK TO:

MY FINAL CRAZY DRAWING:

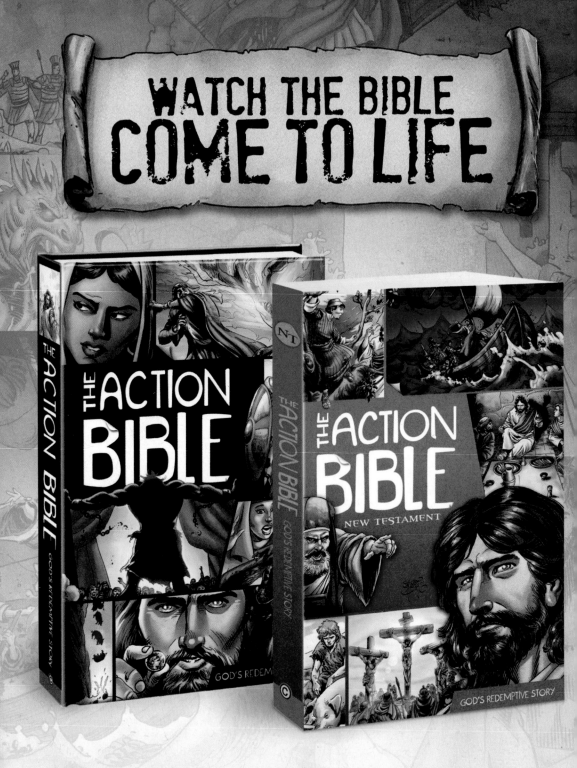